KNIGHT
OF
Penn Quarter

Book 9 of the Knights of the Castle Series

Terri Ann Johnson and
Michele Sims

To a Tee Publishing
Washington, D. C.

Knights of Penn Quarter by Terri Ann Johnson and Michele Sims
Copyright@2020

Digital ISBN: 978-1-952871-07-8
Trade Paperback: ISBN: 978-0-578-81628-9

To a Tee Publishing
Washington, D.C. 20019

Cover Designed by: J.L. Woodson: www.woodsoncreativestudio.com
Interior designed by: Lissa Woodson: www.naleighnakai.com
Editors: Lissa Woodson
Beta: Ellen Kiley Goeckler, Kelsie Maxwell, Debra J. Mitchell, and Bryn Weimer

KNIGHT

OF

Penn Quarter

Book 9 of the Knights of the Castle Series

Terri Ann Johnson and
Michele Sims

♦ DEDICATION ♦

Terri Ann Johnson

I dedicated this book to the tireless efforts of those who work on behalf of enhancing the lives of children here and abroad.

Michele Sims

I dedicated this book to God, the source of all good things and to my loving and patient husband, Tony.

♦ ACKNOWLEDGMENTS ♦

Terri Ann Johnson

First and foremost, I want to thank God for giving me the gifts of life, love, family, health and our Lord and Savior Jesus Christ. Without these gifts nothing would be possible.

To my mom, dad, sister and brother-in-law, who help me when I'm in the writing cave. Thank you for allowing me time to step away from my role as a single mother for a few hours a day to accomplish my goals. And thank you for understanding that the hustle don't stop.

To my son, Joshua, who accepted eating more fast food than he should've while we were quarantined, and Mommy needed to write. Thank you for tolerating my short temper as I bumped up against my deadlines. Most of all, thank you for loving me in the midst of it all.

To my nieces and nephews, Krystal, Phillip, Jr., Christopher, Jr., and Naomi, who always step up when I need you to spend time with your cousin. We love you!

To my brotha, Ronnie Woods, who helped me breathe life into Mateo Lopez. Your insight was invaluable to giving the readers a well-rounded protagonist.

To Rhonda Pope Brown and Nakecia Bowers, who helped me understand the life of a social worker and everything they go through to help make this world a better place to live.

To all of my friends, who understand that I can't talk as often as normal because I'm typically writing.

To the Zoom writing crew, particularly Jeida Walker and Victoria Adams-Kennedy, thank you for encouraging us to set time aside, daily, to fulfill our dreams. Thank you to Michelle Rayford, Nikko Michelle and Lachelle Weaver for staying up with me into the wee hours of the morning to hit our writing word counts for the day.

To London St. Charles for helping to plot the story. Your energy is contagious.

To my editor, Naleighna Kai, for challenging me to improve the novel and for your tireless energy.

To Karen Bradley, Debra Mitchell, Ellen Kiley Goeckler, Brynn Weimer and Kelsie Maxwell, the best beta readers this side of Jordan. Thank-you for your comments and corrections. J.L. Campbell and Candice 'Ordered Steps' Johnson, I appreciate your creativity with assisting us with branding. Thank-you to the NK's Tribe Called Success for the accountability and motivation to keep going.

To J.L. Woodson, thank-you for the awesome cover. Your work is phenomenal.

Thank you to Victoria Christopher Murray and ReShonda Tate Billingsley for giving this novice writer a chance to fulfill her dream of becoming an author.

To my Sistah in Greekdom and in the pen, Michele Sims, this has been an awesome ride. Thank you for working to get this novel where it needed to be.

To each and every reader and book club, thank you for your support. I hope you enjoy this romantic suspense.

Michele Sims

I'm grateful to Naleighna Kai for presenting the idea of a collaboration with my sister of the pen, Terri Ann Johnson. Terri, we clicked from the start and creating this story with you was a pleasure. I would also like to thank my family members and dear friends for their support of my writing career. J. L. Woodson, your covers for this book and each book in the Moore Family Saga are awesome. To Karen Bradley, Debra Mitchell, Ellen Kiley Goeckler, Brynn Weimer, Christine Pauls, and Kelsie Maxwell, thank you for your valuable input. Thanks also goes out to NK Tribe Called Success, members of the NAMAKIR and NAMISTE Tribes. A special thanks to J. L. Campbell for your assistance with marketing. And to you, my dear readers, thank you all for your love and support.

Chapter One

Agent Mateo Lopez, known as "El Gato", the cat with many lives, decided that neither curiosity nor his career with the FBI would be his cause of death.

Despite telling the agency that he was done, here he sat as his supervisor poured over his personnel service record planning to send him into danger, yet again.

"You're an accomplished agent and I see why you've earned your code name. I can't imagine it's your intent to give up your outstanding career at this point." His supervisor, Janice Clark said, sliding his file to the top of the pile on her desk.

"Intent?" His throaty sounds mimicked laughter, except it left a bad taste in his mouth and was tinged with bitterness. "If a man is lucky to escape one close call after another, he has a chance to think about things. It was never my *intent* to be in my grave before the age of thirty-five."

He should've walked straight to Human Resources and turned in his early retirement papers after the last FBI undercover operation went terribly wrong. He was done with everything about this place, and his blood boiled as he sat in Agent Clark's office, having to debate about what was best for him.

"It's been a long morning already," she said. "I think I'll have a cup while we discuss this matter."

Observing her deliberate attempts to placate him as she walked over to the Keurig, he knitted his brow and sighed while she took her time searching through different flavors of coffee and finally inserted a pod into the machine.

"Agent Lopez, I'll need you on this one."

Undeterred in his decision to get out of the office as soon as possible, he observed her while she stood in front of the coffeemaker. As it gurgled, she smiled and inhaled the aroma of the strong brew filling the air.

"I'd like to give you more high-profile assignments."

"More cases? Sounds interesting, Agent Clark, but as I said, I'm done."

"Hear me out," she implored. "I can make sure the assignments are in exotic locations so that you can mix business and pleasure." Wiggling her eyebrows, she gave him a sly, all-knowing smile.

Mateo's ten-year career with the FBI had its ups and downs, but the last operation had rocked him to the core. His answer was still no.

"After everything that's happened, even that carrot doesn't appeal to me. Besides, it's time for me to do my own thing."

"I know you still have bad feelings about the last operation—"

"Bad feelings," he shot back. "Is that what you're calling it?"

She reclaimed her seat behind the huge mahogany desk which swallowed her petite frame. At five feet and two inches tall, she often kept her blond hair tied in a tall bun on top of her head to add an additional inch to her height. She was probably in her mid-sixties but didn't look a day over fifty-five. Janice knew her stuff and she took as much as she gave. Understanding the old boy mentality that still operated throughout the agency, she knew how to play the game; most of the time, she won.

"You still haven't heard me out."

"I'm listening, Agent Clark." Studying her with a laser focus, he wondered about *her* intent.

Two years had passed since a dirty agent had accused Mateo of teaming up with the Sanchez drug cartel in Mexico and setting their ground operation on fire to get rid of evidence. It was the same drug cartel which was responsible for importing a huge amount of cocaine and guns into the United States for at least five years, possibly more. Mateo was the first agent the FBI was able to use to infiltrate the organization and get information that could incriminate them. Unfortunately, once the real rat, Agent Fletcher, accused Mateo of conspiring with the enemy, he'd been arrested and charged, spending a few days in jail until his arraignment.

Anger tap danced on the outskirts of his mind as he thought of the toll being arrested and wrongly accused took on him and his family. If it wasn't for Carlos Rivera at the DEA, a lifelong friend, who had also infiltrated the organization and provided the proof of his innocence, he might still be behind bars.

The spirit of El Gato was destroyed by this agency. He died waiting in that jail like a common criminal. He frowned and her voice brought him out of his thoughts.

"You know we dismissed Agent Fletcher after lying about what happened on the op."

"That's the least that should've happened." Mateo leaned back in his chair and unbuttoned his jacket. "Why me? I've been training the recruits since then and I'm not trying to go back out in the field."

Mateo reached into his wallet, pulled out one of his business cards, and offered it to her. "Everyone in this unit has heard me talking about my company, Global Connections Security. I'm ready to get back out there, but this time on my terms and with a crew I can trust."

Mateo didn't care how she took the news as he shared what had been on his mind for a long time.

In her silence, he continued, "I've been loyal to the FBI for years, played by the book, and still I was arrested as if I couldn't be trusted. I'm curious as to why you want someone that you don't trust to continue working for you?" He crossed one slack-covered leg over the other, and waited for her answer.

"I had your back every step of the way," she replied. "This entire department did. And yes I'm asking you to come back, because you still have a lot to offer. You're one of my best agents."

"I couldn't tell," Mateo huffed.

The nonstop undercover assignments had wreaked havoc on Mateo's personal life. Although he witnessed small crimes, he let them go in an effort to accomplish the larger goal. Getting caught in one crisis after another, he knew it was by his own wits and survival skills that he made it out alive. As much as Mateo wanted to feel as though he was putting a dent in some of the illegal activities assigned to him, he ended up feeling as though he was paddling upstream in rough waters without an oar.

Yet, he had chosen this life and knew from the beginning that being undercover presented multiple issues that kept many agents single. In the undercover game, agents made enemies, and he didn't want to fall in love with someone and cause them to become targets. So, he distanced himself from his blood family to keep them safe hoping they understood.

However, when it came to women, he had to be honest and accept that he loved the company of beautiful women who, too many times, used him for the perks of his job. They loved meeting him in exotic places where his assignments took him; the wining and dining in expensive restaurants as a part of his cover. They were misguided about the big government paycheck they thought agents received, without realizing that they were public servants and not rolling in cash. Mateo made it clear to them, ensuring they understood anything they did as a couple wasn't serious, just fun.

"I know that the last op caused you pain, in more ways than one," Agent Clark insisted. "But you were trained and experienced enough to deal with the pressure."

"Facts." Mateo nodded, but he was burned out and wanted to run his own company. His full-time job interfered with his dream.

Mateo recalled the time when he was first approached to work on the Sanchez Cartel operation. They needed someone with his background and knowledge of San Miguel de Allende, Mexico, where his parents were born and only twelve hours from Laredo, Texas. He'd only visited a few times as a child and saw it as an opportunity to give back to his ancestral home and reconnect with old friends like the Rivera family who now lived one hundred and seventy miles away in Mexico City. He felt certain that after so many years, no one there would recognize him as a grown man. Because he was skilled as an agent and had thorough knowledge of the people and their customs, he was assigned the lead instead of Agent Fletcher who was senior to him.

Agent Fletcher had done everything he could to ensure that it wasn't a success.

Mateo shifted in his seat as he verbalized his thoughts about the man he had believed to be a trusted colleague, but turned out to be his chief nemesis.

"Trust me, he won't get a job as a dog catcher in this country." She folded her hands on her desk and leaned in. "We've made sure of that."

At this point, Mateo funneled his energy into working with new recruits. This gave him the opportunity to pour into their spirits the character of a real agent. Maybe that was what Agent Fletcher had been sorely missing.

"What is it that you need from me and what exactly are you asking?"

Her brown eyes widened as she sipped her coffee. "We've gotten wind that there's an illegal operation involving a child services agency in the city. They're using foster kids to run drugs for them. They pay the foster parents extra money as an incentive. Unfortunately, there are also allegations of sex trafficking."

News like that made Mateo recall some of his bleakest times as an agent. "And you want me to go in and do what?"

Agent Clark pulled a folder from her desk and propped it open. "This is the man we believe is responsible for the connection between the criminal enterprise and the Loving Our Babies Social Services Agency." She slid a picture across her desk to him.

Mateo peered at the black and white glossy photo and thought he may have recognized the face, but he was uncertain where they may have met. "Again, what are you asking me to do?"

"We'd like you to bring them down. Everything we know about the operation is in here."

He slid the picture next to the folder, leaving both on the the desk and eased out of the chair.

"I've spent twenty minutes longer in here than I intended. Thanks for the information, but I'm not promising I'll do anything with it." Smiling thinly, he turned toward the door.

"Think about it and let me know," she shot back, unmoved by anything he said.

"I'm headed to Human Resources to submit my early retirement paperwork Agent Clark."

"Even if you do that today, you still have forty-eight hours to rescind it."

"Sometimes in life you have to follow your spirit, and I only stayed this long to make sure that I have my pension."

Seeing that the conversation was over, she rose and watched as he walked away.

"You can't fault me for trying."

"I don't. Goodbye." He left the office and looked down the hallway at the entrance to the Human Resources office. He couldn't shake the image of the man in the folder. The shivers coursing down his spine concerned him; which was never a good sign.

Chapter Two

"Do you realize that I have a caseload of over sixty-five families?" She protested. "How am I to protect the children from imminent danger with so many cases to handle?"

Rachel Jordan glared at her supervisor as frustrations mounted to the point where she drew in an angry breath.

"Do I realize it?" Jake Lowery smirked, which only increased her irritation with him and her situation. "Of course. I gave you the caseload and if you don't stop complaining, you'll have more." His lips tightened in response and she flinched under his unsympathetic gaze. "You have one of the lightest caseloads in the office and you're the last one hired. I've been patient with you, but you know everyone here has to pull their own load."

She rounded her desk, now covered by the additional stacks of folders he had brought in, and made her way to the grey file cabinet. Its steel drawers were teeming with folders and required effort to pry it open. When she'd arrived, her case files were so disorganized that her first task was to organize them alphabetically by the family's last name and highlight the tabs in red, yellow, or green based upon the severity of the child's situation. Fridays had become her day to stay in the office to update her cases by color code, while other young professionals headed to local establishments in the city for happy hour. Penn Quarter's vibrant nightlife offered music, dancing, and restaurants of diverse cultures. Unfortunately, Rachel rarely had the time or pleasure to indulge.

"It's not just my active cases, do you see all of this?" She waved her hand over the files in a Vanna White motion. "I came here, and it was as if I was dropped in an emotional Armageddon with very few people to lend any help." She lowered her hand by her side. "Yes, I was the last hired, but it was also clear that some of the most difficult cases were transferred to me to handle and I did it."

Although uncomfortable speaking about her accomplishments, she knew she had to say something. Despite the challenges, she had maintained a commitment to the organization and had successfully placed more children in homes than most of her peers. But with every successful case she closed, she was given cases that merited two red tabs because they were in the most danger. Those were the cases that landed many a caseworker on the wrong side of the unemployment line.

She rubbed her forehead as she pleaded her case trying to stem the throb of a headache. "Also given the fact that I've established myself and have a proven track record, I still fear that with too many cases, my reputation could be diminished. That will leave me accountable and possibly blamed for something that happened beyond my control."

Jake shifted his body from side to side. "You worry about things too much Rachel."

"I have to be concerned. You know that I don't treat my clients as though they're just another number," she countered, leveling a hard glare. "You know I spend time with the families, and I see their hurt, their pain, and the anxieties they have about their futures."

Jake grimaced and averted his gaze to the playground outside the window. He had hired Rachel as an adoption social worker for a nonprofit agency, Loving Our Babies. Her primary role was to facilitate the process for both the adoptive family and for the child who was being adopted. When she graduated from the University of the District of Columbia fourteen years ago with a master's degree in social work, she was hopeful about her ability to make a change in the lives of others and had looked forward to a bright beginning in her professional life. That optimism was waning on a daily basis.

"As long as you keep your cases handled and out of the news, you can look at them anyway you want." Jake sipped his coffee, the way he liked it, black from a flimsy paper coffee cup. The dark brew seeped through the seams of the cup and dripped down the front of his white shirt leaving stains.

God doesn't like ugly.

He tried to wipe the brown stains away and his sloppiness irked Rachel. She hoped he would leave her space so she could get a handle on all the work he'd taken from others and not tactfully gave to her. Instead of continuing the discussion at this time, she reclaimed the slightly worn seat behind her desk, opened the desk drawer, and pulled out a few napkins. She offered them to him, although she wasn't sure if he even cared about his stained shirt.

"There's the James case that I haven't checked on in a while," she said, realizing the new cases meant her workday would be longer and the attention she could pay to others would diminish. "And a case in South Carolina—"

"Then you need to go and check on them," he shot back with a shrug. "We don't have any money for a plane ride, but you can take the train to South Carolina and leave the James case to me; I'll check on them."

Although Jake was rough around the edges and a tough supervisor, Rachel treated him as if he were the grumpy uncle who was smart and mostly helpful in navigating office politics. In five years, she planned to be in his position. She'd stayed at her first job for nearly ten years and that was only because they paid for her advanced degree. But this one was all about her future.

"Which one are you thinking about visiting?" Jake peered at her for a moment.

She remained silent, contemplating as she placed a pen to her lips. "I'd prefer to visit the James family in Northeast. I've connected with the children and I'd like them to see my face more often."

"You're not supposed to get too close, remember to remain objective, Rachel," he spat, seemingly annoyed that she would disregard what he said earlier.

"You asked and that's my choice. I would appreciate it if you'd think about it over the weekend. Then let me know on Monday if you still want me to go to South Carolina."

Jake grumbled something that she couldn't quite make out. He frowned and got up from his seat.

"Before you go, may I have permission to leave a little early? You know, in the event I have to travel next week?"

His eyebrows winged upward as Rachel shifted her ponytail from one side to the other. "You're pressing the issue. You'll have time to complete travel requests only if I decide you're going to go."

"I can't represent us if I don't have myself together."

Jake's dry lips split into a grin. "Well, it may depend on your answer to my question."

"What's your question?" Rachel tilted her head, feeling like she was about to be set-up.

"Angie's birthday is on Monday. Can you bring lunch for the office?" he asked, rubbing his hands together with anticipation. "My wife left today for a girls' trip and I hoped you could whip something up over the weekend...while I meditate about my answer."

Rachel was right. Pure setup. She was known as the office chef who tried recipes of various cuisines from around the world. In return for a free sumptuous meal, they kept the candy jar on her desk filled to the brim with chocolate kisses. She discovered that the old saying, the way to a man's heart was through his stomach, was still true as several men in the office asked her out on dates after enjoying one of her lunches. She always refused, as a broken heart from a prior relationship left her unwilling to take a chance on re-opening the wounds that took much too long to heal.

"I can whip up something," she said. "And I'll bring enough for the office on Monday. But for all of that hard work that answer needs to be a 'yes'."

Jake gave a slight bow. "My taste buds and my stomach thank you. Peace out."

She shooed him out of her office and freshened up a new shade of pink lipstick which complemented her sienna complexion.

Scanning her office with the additional files on her desk and the ones on the floor caused reality to set in. Leaving early and keeping everyone satisfied with her good food didn't lessen the tinge of loneliness that typically set in on Fridays.

Rachel was given more to do this morning than anticipated, and didn't feel good that she was hiding behind her work instead of moving on with her life. She couldn't keep going on like this knowing that burnout was real. For now, she needed to organize her home visits as she glanced at the mounds of files growing in her office like a wayward plant. Rachel prided herself on not missing obvious things even if she wasn't afforded the time or opportunity to analyze the situation. That's where some of her colleagues had landed in trouble, with reporters sniffing out the story after things went terribly wrong.

Rachel rose to complete the task of filing the last few cases before she hit the door for the weekend. Everyone in the office knew that Friday evenings were Rachel's time to organize. She was thankful that no one would disturb her. She opened her desk drawer and grabbed her phone. After locating the Sirius XM app, she connected it to the Bluetooth speaker. Sirius XM's Heart and Soul station blared through her office. Once she made it to the bottom of the stack Rachel noticed a file that wasn't marked with her color-coding system. She recognized it as Felicia Smith's case, the Hart family in Southeast, DC. Jake reassigned the case from Rachel to Felicia a few months ago. Rachel met the children and had them taken to their foster home with Mr. and Mrs. Williams. She couldn't fathom why Jake would assign three children to Felicia because she neglected her cases and he stayed on her regarding follow-up. Her commitment to her cases was abysmal and her work ethic, inferior.

As Rachel opened the folder, a note fell to the floor. She picked it up and grew increasingly angry as she read it.

"Hi Rachel. I hate to ask you this, but I plan to call out on Monday. Child Protective Services will conduct a wellness check for the Hart children on Monday morning. Can you meet them at the house at nine am? I'm sure that everything will be fine. I owe you one. Oh, and please don't mention this to Jake. I'd rather ask for forgiveness than permission. Thanks, Felicia."

Really?!

"Calm down Rachel. You're doing your best under difficult circumstances." She repeated the mantra but couldn't shake the dreaded feeling that something awful had already happened.

Chapter Three

Sensing she needed some relief from the heavy weight of responsibilities on her shoulders, and also realizing the likelihood that she would bite someone's head off if she didn't get out of there, Rachel left the office early. She planned to sit with her beautician for a few hours of pampering and self-care.

"You have magic hands, Leticia." She closed her eyes as the warm water and rhythmic squeezing of her hairdresser's fingers massaged her scalp.

"Hey Brenda." Leticia looked up and welcomed her next patron.

"Hey Ticia, I'm early. Anya told me to let you know she'll call you to get in as soon as possible. She has an invitation to the Telfair wedding this weekend.

"The Telfair wedding?" She let out an appreciative whistle. "That's got to be one of the events of the year. And with the Lewis wedding coming up, as well, I've been swamped." Leticia stopped massaging her scalp for a few seconds and Rachel frowned at the interruption. "I'll be sure to save her a spot. Have some refreshments in the lounge, and I'll be right with you." The woman sauntered away.

"Rachel, your neck muscles are so tight," Leticia said, getting back to work. "Have you been busier than usual at work?"

"Yes," she sighed and said no more about it. Leticia had been her hairdresser for years and knew when not to press the issue of work with Rachel or disturb her peace. She engaged in less chit chat and focused on applying her skills as a hair professional, making sure Rachel was pleased with the results.

She left the beauty shop relaxed and looking like a fashion model with bouncy curls. Rachel took the metro train to her home which was her sanctuary in Penn Quarter. She didn't regret signing the lease on the seventh-floor apartment a little over a year ago, even though it was a major drain on her income.

Time had flown by and it was already eight o'clock when she kicked off her shoes in the foyer and placed her bag on the glass dining room table. She stared at the view of the Washington Monument through the two Cathedral windows as she walked toward the balcony. She loved this space, her little piece of heaven, as much as the first day she laid eyes on it. Rachel never closed her drapes because the view was the reason she settled on leasing this particular apartment.

She headed to the bathroom for a quick shower and a night in her favorite purple silk pajamas. Before opening a bottle of Chardonnay, she prepared a mixed green salad with leftover rotisserie chicken, a plate of fresh goat cheese, and crackers drizzled with honey. She hummed a tune while attending to her task, but also had a nagging thought of why Jake was so insistent about handling any of her cases. He never liked to do any of the heavy lifting.

Friday evening was her special time to rejuvenate after a long week of juggling client cases. She settled on the couch, pulling a fleece blanket over her legs before grabbing her firestick from the side table and streaming her favorite series. Only once did the idea of having someone to share moments like this, come to mind.

Within an hour, she dozed off to sleep. All the aggravation and anxiety that she felt earlier had been swept aside.

* * *

"Another gorgeous sunrise." Rachel packed her car with Asian fare of Thai shrimp and dumplings she prepared during a weekend of TV binging, exercising, and sleeping.

Rachel admired the orange and yellow autumn leaves of the trees that lined the sidewalks. She removed her jacket as it wasn't as cool this early November day as she'd anticipated. She arrived at work earlier than most of her co-workers, breaking in the cooking utensils she purchased from La Cocina, a new shop that opened last month in Penn Quarter.

After laying out the office's lunch, she went to her office and retrieved the files that she'd need. Rachel returned to the employee break room where she was greeted by Lachelle Jackson sampling a few of those lunch portions for breakfast.

"Good morning, Lachelle. Are you going to leave some of those for the rest of us?" She asked, taking in the fact that her friend was putting a major dent in the food. She went to the refrigerator to grab a drink before heading to the round table near the vending machine.

"Hello Rachel," Lachelle said with a mouthful. "These Thai Shrimp and dumplings are amazing. When did you have time to make these this weekend?" Dabbing the corner of her mouth, she finished chewing and grinned like she'd just won the Powerball. "And enough for the whole office, at that."

I have nothing but free time on the weekend. "Won't be enough the way you're laying into them."

"Sorry. I'll wait for lunch." Lachelle slid the cover over them.

"You didn't care what they were for," Rachel teased, bringing a smile to her friend's face. "To answer your question, I've made these before. It wasn't hard, and didn't take long to prepare. I like to experiment with new recipes in my free time." She gestured to the assortment on the rectangular table in the break room. "I also brought fruit and assorted muffins for a continental breakfast."

Rachel tightened her lips and hoped Lachelle wouldn't launch into *what else did you do this weekend* line of questions.

Having served as the Program Director for Loving Our Babies agency and in various other roles over fifteen years, Lachelle had been excited when Rachel reached out and asked her to be her mentor. Ten years Rachel's senior, Lachelle was like a sister in addition to her Director. She had taught Rachel how to balance the fine line of being professional while being caring and respectful to her clients. Since most of their clients were young, Rachel provided the connection they needed with someone closer in age.

"Are you still planning to make a few home visits today?" Lachelle asked, shifting her focus to the chocolate croissants. "I needed to talk to you, and I've cleared my schedule for at least an hour."

"Okay, but I had to add another to my schedule after Felicia called out this morning," Rachel said while retrieving clear dessert plates from her bag. "I have a wellness visit on the Hart children, so I plan to leave shortly. Can I call you while I drive to meet Child Protective Services?"

"Sure. It's better we talk when I'm behind a closed door." Lachelle scanned the room quickly and paused as another employee entered the room; a woman who could spread office gossip quicker than a California wildfire.

* * *

"I'm concerned about the Hart children with the Williams family," Lachelle said after Rachel connected the call to her through the car's Bluetooth function. "It appears some neighbors have accused the foster parents of using the kids to sell drugs."

"Really?" Rachel exclaimed. "What kind of people would mistreat children who already ended up on the rough side of life?"

"People who know the system is overloaded and the chances of being caught is small." Lachelle let out a long, weary sigh. "Child Protective Services will get the kids out of there if they find evidence that warrants it, then the courts will place them in emergency housing. It is my understanding that CPS may be on the scene when you get there. I was told by one of my sources there that a team of investigators had been dispatched to the home where the Hart children were placed."

A deflated sigh escaped Rachel's lips. "The stress of this job."

"Let me share something with you on a more pleasant note. I've been thinking about, or should I say, John and I have been thinking about..." John Braxton, a retired professional athlete, was Lachelle's fiancé. They had been engaged for about a year.

"What's up?" Rachel reached over and grabbed a Hershey's kiss from the bag in the console between the driver and front passenger seat.

"You know I talk to him about my co-workers; the good, the bad and all of the ugly."

"And I'm a part of the good, I'm guessing."

"Yes, ma'am. You are." Lachelle cleared her throat and continued, a sure sign she was gearing up for something Rachel wasn't going to like. "John loves your cooking and he thinks you're a sweetheart."

Rachel furrowed her brow feeling a setup before it passed her friend's lips. "Uh oh. Where is this going?"

"There's someone we'd like to introduce you to."

Rachel turned the music down and then put her attention back to the road filling with morning traffic.

"Really?" She smirked, knowing there was zero interest in a blind date of any kind.

A few guys, whom she had gone out with, presented themselves as gentlemen. Then after a few dates, their authentic selves showed up setting one new low standard after another. On one occasion, a man expected her to take care of the entire bill after he purposely ordered every high-priced item on the menu. Somehow, he conveniently left his wallet. After that, Rachel ducked into the restroom and slid straight out of the restaurant leaving him to deal with the aftermath.

The dude had the nerve to call her from jail. As soon as she heard the name, she disconnected the line and ditched his number. She was done and refused to take any more of the nonsense. Instead, she dove into the demands of her job, burying herself in work and simultaneously, buried her heart. The casket was closed and locked with soil thrown on it for good measure.

"Girl, listen to me. You're sweet as apple pie and you're the B. Smith of our office. Who else coordinates the birthday gatherings, baby showers, and other special occasions?" Lachelle said, laying out her case. "We'd like to introduce you to someone who is strong, like you are, but also compassionate and kind. You're a natural beauty. Any man would be honored to have you on his arm."

Rachel had always been called a cutie, but she'd tried to dismiss it. Because "cutie" brought unwanted attention from older boys and men looking to exploit girls. Growing up in foster homes, she always wore baggy clothes to deflect that unwanted attention. Her caramel colored complexion combined with dark brown hair that flowed past her shoulders and sparkling brown eyes, often drew unwanted attention.

She tried not to let her mind wander into the incidents that had proven how unsafe she'd been until Lachelle cleared her throat once again.

"What? You want an answer right now?" Rachel laughed as she gripped the wheel.

"You trust me as your mentor on the job, so trust me with this." Lachelle paused for a moment, giving Rachel time to let the statement sink in. "And I, above anyone, can understand wanting to take things slow. But, left to your own devices, you're on the road in the spinsterhood lane."

A lengthy silence fell on the line. Lachelle's husband had been murdered, right in front of her. She'd often told Rachel that God eventually connected her to John, who helped her cope with her grief and who she'd be marrying in less than two weeks. Rachel thought about it for a minute; Lachelle made some valid points. "Okay, I trust you, but you have to tell me more about him."

"We gave Mateo Lopez your number and I'll text his number to your cellphone. Don't worry, you can thank me later."

Rachel's eyes widened as she sputtered over her words. "You...you did what?! But...but Lachelle."

"Bye Rachel," she teased. "And be careful out there."

Call ended registered on the dashboard's display.

Who the heck was Mateo Lopez? And why did they think we'd make a good match?

During the thirty minutes to get to Southeast, DC, through the height of rush hour traffic, her heart thumped against her chest. The GPS signaled that she was half a mile from the house belonging to Mr. and Mrs. Williams, a couple in their middle to late fifties. They had no children of their own and had fostered children before, but only for weeks at a time. The court was grateful when they agreed to provide care for the three Hart siblings, ages seven, ten, and fifteen years old. Caleb and Justice were active boys and the only girl, Heaven, was the oldest.

Her phone rang and she hit accept call and the brakes simultaneously. The tires screeched while coming to an abrupt stop.

"Are you okay? What's going on? I'm calling back to see if you got the number." Lachelle inquired.

"A CPS truck in front of me stopped short and I'm a block away from the Williams' house."

"I'm sure everything will go smoothly," Lachelle said. "They'll just go in and collect what they need, talk to the kids and the foster parents about the allegations, and leave with the kids."

Rachel focused on the house numbers written on the mailboxes. "They're slowing down...the house is probably at the top of the hill."

"Call me and let me know when you're on the way back."

Rachel ended the call and parked on the gravel patch across from the home. She watched as the CPS agents secured their bags, got out of the car, and marched across the street. She stayed behind, scanning the neighborhood and the houses that were so close to each other, someone could reach out of the window of one home and hand the next-door neighbor something through the window.

The silver gate creaked as the lead agent opened it then tripped over the uneven pavement leading to a rusted screen door that fell off the hinges when she pulled the handle.

No answer came after repeated knocks even though two cars were parked in the carport.

Rachel eased out of her car and walked across the street, careful to avoid that little misstep the agent had made.

After three more rapid knocks on the door, the agent called out at the top of her voice. "This is Agent Adams. Open the door. We're here to complete a wellness check on the children."

Those on the outside shared curious looks at the frantic sounds from inside the house of people scurrying around. Rachel could hear the commotion as she maintained her post.

"This is Agent Thompson and we hear you in there. Open the door," warned a tall brown-skinned agent with a deep baritone which echoed through the yard. As he moved closer to the door, Agent Adams stepped to the side to let his burly frame get into position.

Just as he raised the battering ram, a huge pole so heavy that it could barrel through the strongest steel frame, the piercing sound of a gunshot rang out. Screams vibrated so loud Rachel's heart slammed against her chest. Two more quick gunshots, and the door fell into the home at the exact moment that they heard one last gunshot signaling a finality that forced a sob from Rachel's lips.

Chapter Four

Moments seemed like an eternity as the agents backed away from the door seeking cover. They waited for a SWAT-style team to secure the home before entering to find what Rachel feared would be a gruesome scene.

Sirens blared and more officers raced to the scene as Rachel ran back to her car to get her bearings and observe the unfolding crisis. Minutes later, ambulances arrived with stretchers as the first responders administered CPR to two small bodies. Neighbors gathered around at the edge of the property holding each other as some of the women wailed, covering their mouths to hold in the fear.

After the coroner's van arrived and parked in the driveway behind the CPS trucks, Rachel slid out from behind the wheel. No further shots had come after the initial four rang out. Two additional bodies, the length of adults, were transported out of the house covered in white sheets followed by officers speaking into their radios. Others shook their heads, saddened by the terrible turn of events.

Rachel leaned in and gathered her credentials from the car and proceeded up the path to the modest house. She was immediately stopped by a DC police officer assigned to protect the entrance of the home from curious bystanders.

"I'm Rachel Jordan with the Loving Our Babies Social Services Agency," she choked on her words as her gaze blurred from the realization of what just happened to children in her care.

"The Hart children were assigned to our agency and we received an allegation this morning that I came to investigate." She hoped the slight tremor of her hand was not perceptible when she presented her identification to the officer.

"Let me notify the supervisor on site," he said, his voice as solemn as she felt. "I can't give you authorization to go inside."

He returned with a uniformed woman, maneuvering past the swell of people in front of the home, until they made it to where Rachel stood. She turned her head in time to see Lachelle briskly walking toward her.

"I understand you're with the adoption agency," she said, extending a hand. "I'm Officer Walden, the supervisor on site."

"I'm Rachel Jordan and this is my supervisor, Lachelle Jackson. I was here regarding allegations of abuse of the Hart children."

"Please, follow me."

They stepped inside and the metallic smell of blood was almost overwhelming in a home that was too hot for comfort. The officer in charge gave her fellow officer a knowing glance before turning her attention back to Rachel and Lachelle.

"I'm sorry to inform you, but the younger ones, Caleb and Justice died of their wounds ten minutes ago."

"No. No. No. No." The male officer caught Rachel as she swooned upon hearing the news.

"What about Heaven, the oldest child?" Lachelle asked as she nestled her arm under Rachel's to give her support.

"We don't know her whereabouts, but we've launched a search." Officer Walden retrieved a phone from her pocket and stared at the screen a few moments. "I'm sorry but that's all I can share with you at this time."

"Thank you for providing us with that information and we're available if you need assistance with the investigation." Lachelle handed the supervisor one of her cards and after the officers left them at the entryway to join the hustle of activity in the house, Rachel trailed Lachelle back to the car.

"I came as soon as the call came in about the shootings. I'm driving you back to the office."

Numbed by the tragic loss of the children, Rachel was unable to protest as she placed the keys in her friend's hand and settled into the passenger seat.

The drive back was surreal as Rachel thought about the children whom she had met only a few times. Caleb had an infectious smile and Justice, wearing a pair of glasses that seemed to swallow his round face, was inquisitive and loved school. Heaven was a typical teenager and at first had been surly but playful with her siblings as their initial interview had progressed. Rachel saw a picture of their mother April in the files and Heaven had turned into a natural beauty just like her. She had been too addicted to care for her children after she'd lost her job and they became homeless.

Thoughts of *what if* ran through Rachel's mind. What if she had kept the Hart case? What if she'd detected signs of abuse? Would this tragedy have occurred?

Rachel wondered what their lives would have been like if they had gotten a woman like her last foster mother, Sarah Middleton, a retired schoolteacher. Rachel was fortunate to have Mom Sarah. She provided Rachel with love, assistance with school, and the *polish* she needed to take her rightful place among those in the professional world.

Tears flowed as she thought of how much she missed her foster mother, the woman who made such an impact on her life. She cried for the senseless loss of children who had so much of their lives ahead of them. All children like her who were placed in difficult situations through no fault of their own provided the inspiration she needed to continue despite the challenges.

Suddenly, her back stiffened, and she wiped her tears away before they reached the office.

I have to find Heaven. I don't have time for tears.

Chapter Five

A week later, Mateo and Carlos finished a run around the Tidal Basin. Currently painted with fall's vibrant foliage, the area provided a soothing backdrop as they sat on a bench enjoying the view of the Potomac River. Burnt orange, red, and yellow filled the circle around the water, attracting tourists who admired the varying shades of pink cherry blossoms during the spring.

"I'm glad you're back in town, Carlos." He'd been friends with Carlos Rivera before Mateo became an FBI agent, and Carlos, an agent for the DEA. He knew, given the path some of his family members had taken, attending college was his ultimate goal. Since college funds were short, he joined the JROTC in his senior year of high school and was the recipient of their four-year college scholarship. Mateo and Carlos met at their first Army ROTC meeting at Towson State University, located approximately fifty-five miles outside of DC.

During their four years together, they'd often arrived late to their training classes after partying at homecomings and various HBCU bowls. Somehow, they learned the basics of military operation and tactics and as a bonus, they discovered their uniforms attracted the ladies.

They'd charmed Angela Howard, a fellow student, into lending them her car for a few hours so they could drive to another college campus to frolic with other women. They never thought that one of Angela's friends would notice the car outside of the all-female dormitory. Once alerted to their misadventure, she didn't waste any time in getting a ride to the other campus to catch them off guard. Carlos, who was normally conscious of the smallest degree of movement didn't see her walk up behind him as he leaned on the driver's door. She snatched her keys from his hand. His jaw dropped and he didn't have time to alert Mateo, who was still leaning on the back side of the car flirting. When the car screeched from the curb and Mateo tripped and fell to the ground, the crowd howled with laughter. After a few minutes of teasing each other, so did they. Mateo ended up dating her at one point, so all was forgiven. Though they never quite lived down the image of him hitting the ground.

"It's good to be back, but only as a contractor since I retired." Carlos took a swallow of his electrolyte drink and wiped the sweat off his brow before handing the bottle to Mateo. "Are you still planning to put in your papers?"

"I sure am and I'm looking forward to a taste of the good life." He threw back his head and finished the rest of the drink.

"Congratulations on your new house." Carlos patted Mateo on his back. "It's great you were able to purchase it right in the heart of the city."

"Thank you, I appreciate it. I'm a city man and I want to be in the heart of the action. Penn Quarter has the hottest new restaurants and bars."

Carlos nodded. "I can park my car at your house then walk to see the Capitals or the Wizards play. Afterwards, we can bar hop."

They both laughed and gave each other a fist bump.

"Is the Sultan of Armanji still putting you up at the Willard Hotel?"

"Until I move into my new apartment." Carlos smiled at Mateo, his amigo who shared the same olive complexion, dark hair and handsome features and was often mistaken for his brother.

"It must be nice, hermano," Mateo joked, nudging him on the shoulder.

"Si, and don't act as if you haven't experienced perks of the job. Join me there for a drink later tonight."

"I wish I could," he said, standing to gather his things. "But I've got a date."

"Any one I know?" Carlos trailed a few steps behind Mateo to his Chevy Tahoe.

"It's a blind date. So, I can't rightly answer your question." He shrugged as they both laughed.

"Good luck with that."

"I think it'll be fine. Her name is Rachel. My buddy John says she seems like a nice woman."

Carlos bumped Mateo's shoulder and smiled. "Like I said, good luck with that."

* * *

"I hope she doesn't kill me."

The tires screeched as Mateo jammed his brake into the floor of his SUV at the red light. The clock on his dashboard told him he was ten minutes late, which wasn't a good look for a first date. As soon as the light turned green, he accelerated at a speed ten miles over the limit.

Tapping the phone button on his steering wheel, he spoke into the Bluetooth function, "Call Rachel."

The call went directly to her voicemail. He hoped she was running late as well. Two blocks to go and he drove down the street, finally seeing the sign for the Yard House. A sigh of relief washed over him when he noticed his favorite valet standing out front. It was Friday, and a throng of people filled the sidewalks.

"Mr. Lopez, how've you been?"

"I'm good, Jim." He tossed the keys, grabbed his jacket, and entered the revolving door while putting his right arm through his blazer. As he walked away, he realized he left the single red rose on the front seat of his truck.

"Vaya, oh man!"

He stopped in his tracks wondering if he should retrieve it.

As Mateo made a complete turnaround in the revolving door, Jim caught up to him, laughing. "I heard you shouting so I thought you must have left something. I looked on the seat and saw this and I figured it wasn't for me."

"Jim, you're a lifesaver." He took the rose, wrapped in green tissue paper tied in a red bow, from him. Once he made it through the revolving door again, he rushed over to the hostess station.

"Do you have a guest by the name of Ms. Rachel Jordan? My name is Mateo Lopez."

"She's waiting for you. This way please." The friendly hostess told him.

He stopped her before she proceeded to the table. "Pardon me, but can you point her out?"

He wanted to see her before she spotted him. They had exchanged pictures, but sometimes pictures didn't tell the current story. He'd heard enough online dating horror stories to know.

"That's Ms. Jordan over there." She gestured to the woman sitting by herself in a booth surrounded by single tables with couples.

Damn. Her back was to him.

Keep it cool, Mateo. He buttoned his jacket, found his swagger, and followed the hostess to their table.

As he moved closer to the high-backed black leather booth in the back of the restaurant near a massive stone fireplace roaring with flames, the heat caused him to sweat.

"I'll take it from here." He spoke softly to the woman who turned and went back to her station while he took a deep breath, ran his fingers through his hair and stepped forwardto greet his date.

"Rachel Jordan?"

His jaw nearly dropped, and he stood mesmerized in front of the woman whose picture didn't do her justice. Whether it was the effect of the glow from the fireplace complimenting her tea colored complexion, or the swing of dark brown curls over her shoulders, or those alluring brown eyes, he wasn't sure. But he knew he was captivated by her elegance and beauty. The simple black, sleeveless dress was stunning as it exposed the well-toned muscles in her arms. As she placed her wine glass on the table and stood to greet him, he noticed the shapely calves and her ample hips.

He endured the awkward moment of discerning whether they should shake hands or embrace. Laughing out loud, they eventually hugged, wrapped their arms lightly around each other, while he glimpsed over her shoulder at those delicious curves.

"I'm Mateo Lopez." He gave her his most enchanting smile, the one that caused the women he had dated in the past to drop their inhibitions and later their undies if he was lucky.

"I'm Rachel and I'm a hugger."

"I can't tell," he said noting her lips had parted as she gave him a quick surveillance.

I think the lady likes what she sees, and so do I. He took a breath, realizing he needed to clear the air first.

"First, please let me apologize for my tardiness. I had a family emergency and I underestimated the traffic flow. Second," he handed her the rose, "this is for you."

"How sweet. Thank you." She inhaled its scent before taking her seat and placing it next to her phone. He noticed additional things he found enticing, her well-toned legs and manicured toes wiggling in those sexy stilettos.

"Apology accepted and don't worry about being late. I spent the time watching The Wizards beating the Trailblazers." She smirked and then continued. "But we know they can lose a lead in a New York minute."

Rachel pointed to her glass of wine. "Oh, I hope you don't mind that I ordered something to take the edge off. It's been one heck of a week."

"Of course, I don't mind, and I respect a lady who likes a nice drink, a good basketball game, and is confident enough to acknowledge that she's nervous." He sat back, impressed by her already.

Patrons were seated at the bar watching various games on multiple flat screen televisions lined above the lighted liquor bottles and enjoying bar bites. Mateo was starving and planned to have a hearty meal since he'd held off eating until now. The waiter came to the table, filled their glasses with water and left them to review the menu. As they scanned the offerings for the evening, they engaged in the usual introductory small talk about the weather, traffic, and life in DC. As they had spoken a few times, albeit briefly, they knew they were both raised in the city, in different quadrants, and that their age difference was only two years, with Mateo being her senior.

"Refresh my memory?" he asked. "Was basketball your favorite sport?"

"Not just basketball. I love most sports, particularly football, but uhmm… baseball, not so much."

He placed his menu on the table, raising an eyebrow before he spoke. "Have you ever been to a game?"

"The games are too long and from what I've watched, they just don't seem exciting."

"That's why you don't like them; you have to go to a live game. We'll see how you feel several months from now."

Rachel's dark brown eyes rose from her menu to cast her attention on him, causing him to recoil. Evidently she was taken aback that he was already thinking about being with her in March.

"I can't believe that slipped out of my mouth. I know I'm getting ahead of myself."

A faint smile appeared on her face as she resumed studying the menu. "No need to apologize."

"What do you think you'd like to eat? This menu is extensive." He scanned the delicious sounding options.

"I'm not sure. This is my first time here, but I've only heard good things."

"Let me see if I can help." He pointed to a dish on Rachel's menu. "I've had this chicken entrée and it was great."

"It sounds tasty," Rachel said as she nodded her approval.

"Are you ready to order," the waitress with long locs asked before she pushed her red pair of glasses up off her nose.

"I love your glasses," Rachel said.

"Thank you."

Mateo ordered a Corona beer, and then they placed their food orders.

Throwing his arm over the top of the booth, he sat back thinking this was a good time to learn a little more information about each other, especially since they hadn't covered the career aspects of things. He had saved that for last hoping that the issues surrounding the agency she worked for and the allegations would work itself out. The killings of those two children and the foster parents had made headlines.

"You work at Loving our Babies with Lachelle? How do you like it, working with the families that are in such a transition?" He took a sip of his water and leaned closer to her.

"Actually, I love it. It's hard work and it's tiring, but it's also fulfilling." She shifted in her seat and the lighting flickered in her dark brown eyes. "Listen, I don't want to bore you with talk about work tonight, so let's just say that I'm paying it forward."

Tilting his head, he pondered the options.

"I'm not sure what you mean by paying it forward, but when I asked about your family during our last telephone conversation, I noticed you were evasive or changed the subject." Her gaze locked on him as he gave her a piercing look. "You know I'm FBI and we have curious minds." He chuckled as she picked up her glass of water and took a long sip before continuing the conversation.

"There's not much to say, but in the past when I tried to answer the question about my family, either pity or sorrow was the response..." She turned down her lips and looked at him with sad eyes, "or I get the bulging eyes look of surprise when I was honest and said I was raised in many homes in the foster care system. So now I just say I'm paying it forward."

He'd schooled his facial expression to remain neutral as he didn't want her to feel he harbored any negative thoughts about her background.

"I can relate to wanting to pay it forward." He sipped a little of his beer. "My family is originally from San Miguel de Allende, Mexico and my parents moved from there to Columbia Heights right before I was born. I've known many people who would die to get here, and I mean literally. Families are separated and kids end up staying with people who don't mean them any good. In my line of work, I've also tracked down children who were abducted and my team returned them to their families."

She raised her glass. "A virtuous man on a mission."

"And a lady with a purpose." He returned the compliment that they ended with a toast.

She smiled but he noticed a dark cloud stifle her brightness as he reached for her hand. "What's wrong? I didn't mean to say something to make you sad."

"No, it's not you," she whispered. "I just can't get my mind off a case."

"I'm a good listener," he replied, grateful that she hadn't pulled away, but also concerned at the sudden downturn in vibe.

"It's pretty bad and I don't want to cast a cloud over our dinner."

"You can't do that Rachel, not with me." He lasered his attention on her and resisted the urge to sit by her side and pull her into his arms. For a moment, she looked lost, sad even.

"You can't begin something and not finish it. Who knows? I may be able to offer some advice."

She paused and then looked into his eyes. "Alright, but remember you asked for it."

He nodded for her to continue.

"I love each child on my caseload and I really do my best to ensure that they're safe." She picked up her wine glass and swirled the last few sips around before she polished it off.

"By now you've probably heard about the foster parents in Southeast. The murder-suicide. They were assigned to my agency. The case was mine until about six months ago, when it was reassigned to another worker." Rachel flexed her slender fingers around the stem of the empty glass. "I was there that day. I heard the gunshots. This tragedy has been shocking to me."

He kept a supportive hand placed firmly over hers and gave a gentle squeeze. "I'm saddened and sorry to hear that, Rachel."

"My supervisor alerted me to allegations of a foster family using kids to sell drugs. She wanted me to see what I could find out." Rachel shook her head in disbelief. "My co-worker couldn't go to the house that day, but she told me that the wellness check was scheduled. No way was I going to miss the chance to check on them. I wanted to lay eyes on those children and assess things first-hand."

Mateo gave Rachel a reassuring nod. "CPS was contacted to get the kids out of there and the FBI was contacted because of a federal crime. I'm sure DC's finest were alerted too."

"You know the case?" Rachel inquired.

He simply nodded but didn't say more.

"So many agencies had them on their radar," she whispered. "But none of them reached the children in time." Her eyes glistened with unshed tears and he sensed her mood shifting to sadness, so he continued to hold her hand for several silent moments. "When the case was transferred from me, I should've fought to keep it."

"You had no way of knowing that the kids were in a situation so dire."

"It's been a week since it happened, and the oldest child, Heaven, is nowhere to be found. I've driven around several neighborhoods searching for her."

"Now see, that's where I can help," he said, causing her to lock in on him. Finding a missing child was in his wheelhouse. "I can get some of my guys on the case, too. What do you think about that plan?"

"I think it would be awesome," she said, her face brightening with just those words. She paused, taking a deep breath. "It's hard, but I feel if I can find Heaven, I can do something to help her. You know?"

He nodded just before the servers arrived at the table holding up a tray filled with their main courses.

"Maui Pineapple Chicken?"

"That belongs to the beautiful lady." Mateo checked out the contents on the plate. "That looks good."

"And the Ribeye must be yours, Sir."

"Indeed, it is."

The server's arrival with the food lightened the mood, and with a magician's flair he whipped out a pocket-sized flashlight along with a steak knife and handed the knife to Mateo.

"Sir, would you like to check your steak to ensure that it was cooked to your satisfaction?"

Mateo sliced the meat with the precision of a surgeon. "Perfecto."

"Enjoy your meal." The server lifted the tray and the stand and was gone as quickly as he had arrived.

Mateo reached his hands across the table again and fixed his attention on Rachel. "May I bless our food?"

Her gaze narrowed on him as though surprised he would ask.

"You seem surprised. I'm this big FBI guy—"

Rachel stopped him. "Of course. I'd love that." With her hand in his, she allowed him to intertwine their fingers before he bowed his head and she followed by doing the same.

"Father God, we come before you not only to ask you to bless the food that we are about to receive, but to thank you for allowing us to enjoy this time together. We ask that you watch over Heaven and keep her away from danger until we can bring her to safety. Amen."

They raised their heads and a long moment passed before they loosened their grip on each other. Looking into her eyes, he saw respect and admiration as his gaze lingered while unexpected thoughts ran through his head. Maybe, John had been spot on when he said that Rachel could be that someone special that he would never want to let go. Unlike when he first arrived at the table, the physical touch between them wasn't awkward and their belief in a higher power brought an instant connection.

"Mateo, you stared at that steak like you could polish off an entire brontosaurus. I don't want your food to get cold." She gently pulled her hand away and picked up her fork.

"Oh, so you're a Flintstones fan." He glanced at her one more time before slicing into his steak.

After giving her a chance to take the first bites of her meal, he inquired, "Did I make a good recommendation?"

"This is so good." She moaned and took another bite, savoring it. "I love this, but I'll see if I can recreate it at home and put a lil' twist on it."

"And you cook, too?" Mateo chuckled, trying to reign in his thoughts behind that sultry sound that escaped her lips.

"Don't sound so surprised," she said with a laugh. "Women still know their way around pots and pans. I like to try various recipes from different cultures."

"That's great. I'll be waiting for my invitation."

He noticed her shy smile. "Can you cook? You're all up in my skills."

"I can do a lil' sumthin' sumthin' in the kitchen, too. Mi abuela taught me."

She raised her glass. "Women appreciate men who cook and I'm finding out some interesting facts tonight, Mr. Lopez."

After their table was cleared, the waitress appeared with two smaller menus. "Would you like dessert?"

She handed the menu back without looking. "I don't have room for anything else."

"I'm full, too. I'll pass. Can you bring me the bill?"

When this was completed, they eased out of the black wingback booth.

"Do you have your valet ticket?" Mateo asked.

She looked in her purse and handed it to him to pass to the attendant standing at the door. The brisk night air caused her hair to blow away from her captivating face. He gently combed it with his fingers back into its proper place.

"I hope this date isn't our last." He took her by the hands.

"I enjoyed myself," she said, and he was grateful she didn't pull away. "Work consumes most of my time, so I don't have much practice dating anymore. Thank you for putting me at ease. A second date sounds promising."

Her green Ford Escape pulled up to the curb and she went into her purse to grab a tip.

"Do I look like the type of man who would allow his date to pay a tip? I got you."

"Gracias, Senor Lopez," she said with a playful curtsy.

"Of course, Ms. Jordan." They walked a few feet to the car, and he assisted her into the driver seat.

"Text me or call me when you get in. How far do you have to go?"

"Only ten, no more than fifteen minutes with traffic, and I park in a private garage so I should be good." She blessed him with a megawatt smile. "But I'll definitely let you know when I get in."

He wanted to lean down and claim her glossy lips, but he thought better of doing so as it might seem too forward again. He was working on a new, improved version of himself; one who took his time with a woman and understood the importance of romance.

"Drive safely, pretty lady."

A warm feeling stirred and settled in his chest. Call it intuition, but he hoped he would talk to Rachel very soon and their next discussions panned to their dreams, goals, and not only on the child they wished to find.

As he climbed into his car, he wondered less about getting in her bed and instead was curious about what it would be like to be in her heart.

Chapter Six

Rachel awakened to the birds singing as the light of another autumn day shone through her window. She stretched her tired limbs and smiled as she thought about her date with Mateo. Although they'd spoken on the phone before meeting in person, her feelings then were nothing like what she felt after meeting him. He had a strong, powerful edge to him that felt intense despite the fact that he tried to portray a more easy-going vibe. He was a gentleman, and he could cook, too. LaChelle might be onto something.

Although it was still a little dark outside, dawn was Rachel's favorite time of the day. By the time she tidied up in the bathroom and threw on her sweats and tennis shoes, the sun would just be rising over the horizon with its flashy display of bright yellows and oranges piercing through the clouds. She wanted to get at least two miles in before she started her day and that should take her no more than forty minutes.

Smiling as she remembered their date, she was elated their time together had been much more satisfying than she anticipated. Her nerves tingled with excitement all over again with thoughts of being held by him. She recalled how she found the sight and masculine scent of him intoxicating. His swagger was unparalleled, and she liked that he knew how to treat a lady. And yes… Mateo was *fine*. His muscles reminded her of a young Dwayne Johnson, the Rock, and when they left the restaurant, he held out his arm for her. It had been a while since she felt muscles that hard and it was a good thing he held her up because the feel of his strong hand in the small of her back almost caused her to stagger and swoon. Despite attempts to control her response to him, her body pulsed with desire.

Hmm, maybe I should aim for three miles today.

She took the elevator downstairs and once she arrived on the lobby level of her building, she greeted the concierge.

"Good morning Mrs. Luper."

The diminutive gray-haired lady peeked at her watch. "You're a little late this morning, aren't you? I saw you parking close to midnight. You know that's too late for a weeknight."

"I had a very nice date with a respectable young man and time got away from us."

Mrs. Luper pointed a finger and smiled. "Men are nothing but trouble. I've got my eye on you, young lady."

"Thank you." Rachel pulled her hair back in a scrunchie. "Talk to you later."

Rachel started jogging in place, wondering what the old woman would know about trouble. She'd been married for thirty-something years.

"Bye Rachel." Mrs. Luper waved.

She put her ear buds on before taking off. Rachel zipped her jacket up to her neck, wearing an athletic band around her head to warm her ears. Her feet pounded the pavement, first in a slow jog, to get her blood moving. Before she turned the corner, she picked up her pace, and ran past the Whole Foods. The early crew waited in line for the Starbucks next door to open, which she knew would be soon. The aroma of fresh brewed coffee called her name. As Rachel made a right turn onto a smaller, isolated street, she hummed along to the beat of Michael Jackson's *Bad*, playing in her ears.

Maybe that's why she didn't notice the black sedan following her until she was well down the deserted street.

She slowed her cadence and the sedan slowed; she sped up, it did too. Rachel took out her earbuds as fear stirred inside her, quickening her breathing. She turned around and tried to run back down the narrow tree-lined street, but the car climbed the curb, screeching to a halt as she tried to make it back up the block.

A man, shrouded in a black mask and gloves, jumped out of the car. Her reflexes took over as she quickly scanned her surroundings. His eyes widened after she stopped, stood her ground, and positioned her body in a fighting stance. In three rapid strides, the man closed the distance between them triggering memories of unwanted advances by men while in foster care.

Her heart quickened and her body shifted into action. Sweat trickled down her face as he grabbed her left hand with a jerk of his outstretched right arm. After pulling her close enough, she seized the opportunity to jab him in the neck with her other hand.

Remember, hit them in the soft areas. Her trainer's voice slid into her consciousness, empowering her to fight for her life.

The assailant doubled over from the momentum, leaving him writhing in pain after she dealt her final blow with one mighty kick to the groin.

"Get back in the car," another deep menacing voice screamed out as Rachel continued to face her assailant, who struggled to his feet then ambled back to the sedan. They sped off leaving her bewildered and panting as she ran for cover behind the nearest tree struggling to catch her breath.

She was grateful the driver didn't get out and help force her into the car. On a morning with temps that were just above freezing, she wiped her sweaty palms onto her pants. Her chest heaved in an effort to find a normal breathing pattern and she was alarmed when it wouldn't slow down.

Watching as the car sped off in reverse, she pulled the cell from her pocket just as a group of runners turned the corner. Immediately they screamed and scampered out of the way, avoiding the car powering down the street, with no regard for what it might plow into.

"Ma'am are you alright?" A few of the runners made it to her and stood at her side as she crumbled to her knees.

She nodded while replaying the attack in her mind.

"Someone call the police." One of the runners yelled out.

As she leaned back and took in another deep breath, her gut told her that this wasn't a random assault.

Chapter Seven

Mateo was glad she called him, but he couldn't stop his stomach from churning and doing flips as he listened to the detailed account of her attack.

"Are you alright?" He tried to reduce the volume and urgency in his voice so she wouldn't be any more alarmed when she had every reason to be. Further investigation found that the men associated with this case were stone cold killers. He had already petitioned up the chain to have a security detail on Rachel, but that came at the cost of being returned to full active investigation. So, he left that alone.

"Yes, I'm home and I've already given the police a report." As strong as she tried to sound, fear seeped through the phone and it didn't sit well with Mateo. He sighed and rubbed his temples realizing that things were progressing faster than he thought possible. How had those men tied Rachel into anything?

"Tell me, are you really okay?" he asked, softening his voice even more as he conveyed his concern. "After a morning like you've had, it's alright if you're not."

"To be honest, I still feel jumpy and uneasy inside. Several of the runners who came after the attack escorted me home and made sure I got into the building. I feel safe behind my locked doors, but I have no clue why they signaled me out. I'm sorry if I disturbed you but I called Lachelle to let her know I wasn't coming into work today. She made me promise to call you."

He caught the hesitation in her voice, and it registered in volumes. This thing between them was too new for this level of trust. But if her life was in danger, none of that would matter.

"I know we haven't known each other long," he said, choosing his words carefully. "But I want you to know that you're not bothering me. I'm glad you called. Lachelle and John are good people and they know me well. I'm in my car and I was heading to an assignment so…I'm sure Lachelle told you I would probably want to get information while it's still fresh in your mind." He grabbed the steering wheel tighter. "Will you give me permission to come over?"

Seconds seemed like eternity as he waited for her answer while biding his time at a stoplight turning from red to green.

"I'm texting you my address now."

Closing his eyes, relief flooded his thoughts.

"I'm on my way, but I need to warn you that if I see too many bumps and bruises, we're going to have you checked out."

"I'm a little sore," she admitted, "but I don't have any of those. You'll be proud of me, I think, because the guy who came after me can't say the same thing."

A half chuckle escaped when she described how her assailant made his way back to the car like a dog with his tail tucked between his legs.

"I am proud of you and I'll be there in a few minutes. Is it a secure building and will you need to place my name on the visitors' list?"

"We have surveillance and I'll call downstairs to let them know I'm expecting you."

"I'm on my way." He let out a cleansing breath, relieved she had escaped the attempted abduction. But the one thing he knew for sure was that he needed to get to the bottom of the situation. He had been careful in the past not to be seen too often with the same woman, so he had worked long hours and vowed to steer clear of any serious entanglements. Until he met … her.

Was it possible she was targeted because someone saw her with me last night and was trying to send me a message?

* * *

At his knock, Rachel looked through the peephole, and slowly swung the door open.

"Hello Mateo." She moved to the side to allow him to enter her space.

"Good evening, Rachel." He remained planted at the entrance of her apartment and the extended silence between them gave her pause as he looked at her, those soulful brown eyes appraised her as though searching for signs she was more perturbed than she let on. Gently, he tucked those loose strands of hair behind her ears.

"I needed to see for myself that you were alright." His voice was strong, yet sensitive to her distress. She processed the events of this morning with him while trying to remain calm and at the same time slow down the new thoughts racing through her head.

"I'm sorry that happened to you." As his fingers descended, his hand came to rest on her shoulder and he gently pulled her toward him.

She knew she was strong and had been through worse, but nothing prepared her for his kindness and genuine display of concern. Without warning, she felt the sting of salty tears trying to come to the forefront as he pulled her into his embrace and guided her head to the wall of his strong chest. She listened to the comforting beats of his heart, calming her anxiety.

For the first time in her life, she felt what it was like to experience human kindness from a man unattached to a payout of sex or anything else in return. That, in itself, was amazing. Giving her his strength to latch onto. Evidently, she'd been lying to herself. This is the kind of connection she'd been missing out on.

After regaining her composure, she looked into his dark brown eyes which were communicating deep within her soul, his desire to be there for her. As her hands fell to his waist, she felt the hard bulge in his pocket, a concealed weapon next to his badge.

"Can I offer you something?" She wiped her tears with the back of her hand and gestured toward the kitchen.

"No, thank you. I'm fine."

He repositioned them on the couch and asked for a description of her assailant and the vehicle.

"I didn't intend for you to launch your own separate investigation into this. I think the police took my report seriously."

"I'm not doubting the police's plans or intent, but this was a violation, and I don't take kindly to it." A glint of something that could be coldness flickered in his eyes before he looked away. "You're a friend of John and Lachelle and if you mess with my people, you mess with me. That's the code I live by and I don't tolerate social violations," Mateo explained. "If it hadn't been for friends who came to my rescue, I don't know what would have become of me."

"I agree that it's important to have good friends and I'm thankful you consider me one." Her cheeks warmed as she looked up at him.

"I have to make some phone calls, but in the meantime, promise me that you won't go anywhere else today until I can get a handle on this situation." He stood and pulled her up with him. Rachel led him to the door. "I can't have anybody messing with *mi amiga*. I'll call you later, alright?"

"I'll be here. Thanks for coming by to check on me. Goodbye Mateo."

He turned, heading for the elevator, and she closed the door and bolted the locks behind him.

* * *

His first thought was to call Carlos, but he was out of town. The next on his list was his brother from another mother.

He entered his code, dialed the number and waited for Victor 'Alejandro' Reyes who picked up on the second ring.

"Teo. What's up, mi hermano?"

"Aw, look at you, trying to put those Spanish lessons to good use," Mateo teased.

"Dude, members of my family have been speaking Spanish for generations. My Spanish comes naturally. You, on the other hand, are a little suspect."

Although Mateo and Alejandro weren't blood brothers, they felt closer to each other than

some of their own family members. Mateo's aunt, on his mother's side, lived in Chicago and he spent many summers in the Midwest. Alejandro's family lived on the same block as Mateo's Tia Alicia and Tio Marco.

Juan, Mateo's older brother by three years, was closer in age to Dro but whenever they hung out at the basketball court or anywhere else in the neighborhood, their aunt insisted they take Mateo with them.

"Don't leave him here with nothing to do when he can hang out with his big brother," she reminded them. After a period of at least six summers, they never lost touch with each other.

"How's everything in the Chi?" Mateo had adjusted from calling him Alejandro a few years ago. His new crew, The Kings, shortened his middle name to Dro and he preferred it.

"Man, I can't complain. I haven't heard from you in a minute. How's DC treating you?"

He sucked in a heavy breath and thought better of drawing things out. "I met a young lady and had our first date last night." He moved to the window in his bedroom that had a view of the monuments. "She ran into some trouble this morning."

"What happened?"

"Someone tried to rough her up while she was out jogging. She's assuming that it's associated with a case she's working on. She's a social worker and has been out in the streets looking for a runaway, but I'm concerned she may have been targeted because she was seen with me."

"We can't have that," Dro said and there was a shuffle of papers on the other end. "Let me grab something and jot down a few notes."

"I was hoping you and The Kings could assist in some way. I'm still planning to retire from the FBI, and I don't want to arouse any suspicions by using my sources at the agency to find out information. At this point, after I declined to extend my time, they also didn't give the okay to afford her some protections."

"No need to worry. The Kings are in and I got you."

The Kings, a powerful group of men brought together by one man. Dro's mentor in Chicago, Khalil Germaine, escaped an assassination attempt on his life and afterwards, a group of Khalil's mentees, including Dro, organized a plan to find the culprits, despite the danger to each of them and their loved ones. Over a six-month period, they created a bond of trust among them and branded themselves *The Kings of the Castle.* Their reach was even broader than any government agency.

"We can definitely assist, but what did you have in mind?"

"Rachel, that's her name, is a strong woman but I want her whereabouts tracked in case the attackers return or something else goes down." He thought his request might sound a little awkward, so he explained, "I'm not into stalking her but I know one of your fellow Kings is a tech guru. He has gadgets that I can't get my hands on at the FBI."

Dro was silent for a moment.   "I thought you were on your way out to do your own thing?"

"I was, but I discovered there were connections between the case my supervisor was trying to have me look into and one on Rachel's caseload. There are allegations about a foster family using children to sell drugs."

"Man, you're telling me we're talking about a crew that has children selling drugs."

"That's what I said. I told them I was in for this one last case, but they threatened to limit my resources until I agreed to sign on for more. I declined, and it only confirmed that it was time to do my own thing."

"I feel you on that."

"Any ideas, Dro?" He held his breath hoping that Rachel would agree to whatever plan they devised.

"We have many options, but a tracking device is a good one. Daron, my Brother King over at Morgan Park, handles our high-tech security and tracking devices. If we can dream it, he can conceive it. He's a genius."

"I feel better after talking to you, but I'll need to talk to Rachel also."

Mateo grabbed a shirt off the bed and pulled it on over his head.

"I understand and I know how independent women are these days, especially the good ones. I suggest you make it seem like it's her idea."

He laughed. "That's some good advice right there. I'll give it some thought."

"Let me put one more thing on your mind before I get down to business with finding the best device for your girl."

Mateo smiled, as he liked the sound of Rachel being his girl.

"What's up?"

"If you're serious about that early retirement from the FBI, I'd like to talk to you about working with The Kings on a few missions. I know your expertise and you wouldn't work for us, but with us, as a brother, a Knight."

Mateo remained silent for a moment as he contemplated Dro's offer.

"Bro, no one wants me to chill, relax, get some R and R..." He rubbed his chin and didn't put up too much resistance as the idea of working with Dro intrigued him.

"You've got my attention. Tell me more."

"I know your worth, Teo, and we're always glad to add people like you to our team. You know it's hard for me to trust folks besides you, The Kings, and close family members. You're my brother from another mother and father, if we want to be truthful. I'd trust you with everything I have. That's how we've always rolled. Think about it and we'll still talk later. We have time."

"Thanks, Dro. I owe you one."

"There's no debt between brothers. Adios."

Mateo disconnected the call and tossed the phone on the bed. How was he going to sell his idea to Rachel? More importantly, how much time did he have to get her to a safe place?

Chapter Eight

"Uncle Mateo!" Maria Lopez dashed from her group of friends as they walked from the church's sanctuary to the fellowship hall where the party in her honor would be held. While laughing with a few of his cousins, Mateo's tall figure caught her attention. Her long glossy hair flung behind her as she ran to meet him.

"You didn't miss the Mass, did you?"

He leaned down and planted a kiss on her forehead. "There's no way in the world I'd miss any part of your Quinceanera." The Lopez family celebrated Maria's fifteenth birthday with the traditional Hispanic coming of age celebration. The soirée was reminiscent of a debutante ball but with the added flair of Mexican culture.

Mateo loved his niece and his eighteen-year-old nephew, Miguel. He had always treated them as if they were his own. As Maria stood before him, thoughts of taking them to Adams Morgan Day, a yearly carnival in the Columbia Heights section of the city, ran through his mind. Even though Miguel was three years older than Maria, they would fuss over who would sit on top of his massive shoulders to view the colorful floats and school bands marching in the street. He even kept two beds in his extra guest room, as they'd often have movie nights after their daytime adventures.

"Maria, come on over so you can change into your next outfit," Camila, Mateo's sister-in-law, called out. She rushed over and reached out for a quick hug.

"Go on in, Maria. I'll see you in a few minutes." He watched as she picked up her teal blue ball gown from the ground and trailed behind her mother.

Mateo turned to finish conversing with his cousins while everyone was busy preparing for the lavish show and dinner.

Juan, his brother, bumped into him. "What's up G man?" Juan was shorter and rounder than Mateo. Always the bullying big brother, he slapped Mateo on the back just a little too hard. "It's been a while since we've seen you up in this part of town."

Over the years, Juan never concealed his angst regarding the fact that his younger brother was a FBI agent and seemingly more successful. Their bond as brothers remained strong as Mateo respected that Juan had a dark side, but still loved and supported his family. He'd been a mechanic since graduating from high school. With a steady income, he was able to give his brood a house with a white picket fence and a fur baby.

Juan's envy subsided, albeit a little, after Miguel started running with the wrong crew to try his hand at becoming a corner boy. Miguel was arrested for possessing illegal drugs and Mateo pulled some strings with Carlos to get Miguel off with reduced charges and a slap on the wrist. Juan knew the head of the crew and paid him a visit, vowing to kill him if he so much as looked at his son again.

Mateo was aware his big brother rolled with the criminal element that controlled certain parts of the city and that was the main reason he didn't come around very often. The less he knew, the better. But today was a day to celebrate and he'd try to stick to that script.

"I can't thank you enough for everything that you did for Miguel," Juan said as he shifted his tone from joking to serious. "I want my son to be more than I am, and that kind of trouble could've cost him his future. And you know Mom and Dad would have been disappointed and blamed me." Juan and Mateo's parents left DC for their home in San Miguel de Allende, Mexico after raising their sons in a loving two parent household. They took the chance on migrating to the United States in an effort to give their children more than they ever had. But the need to care for ailing, elderly family members called them back home.

"Mi familia is everything to me," Mateo responded as he rested his hand on Juan's shoulder. "You know how much my niece and nephew mean to me. I'd move heaven and earth for either of them."

Juan allowed himself a grin. "Let's go in."

"Yeah, you know I'm ready to reenact the scene in Bad Boys when Will Smith and Martin Lawrence scared his daughter's date," Mateo admitted as Juan doubled over in laughter. "I'm serious, I can't take seeing all of these boys hanging around my niece. I've been waiting for this for fifteen years, bro."

Juan slowed down and averted his gaze as they made it closer to the entrance of the party. "Before we go in, I want you to know that if you ever need anything, and I mean street wise, let me know. I still have some juice out here."

"Gracias, but I'm knocking on retirement's door, almost banging it down. I think I'm good."

Juan nodded as he said, "Keep it in your back pocket, bro…keep it in your back pocket."

Mateo didn't realize that the day he'd need to pull that favor from his back pocket would be sooner than he'd ever imagined.

Chapter Nine

John and Lachelle's wedding day finally arrived, and at the insistence of the bride and groom, Mateo and Rachel agreed to attend the ceremony together. Mateo had called earlier to tell her he wanted to talk about something before they made it to the church.

"Now? I'm too excited for John and Lachelle to focus on anything else today," she explained. "I promise we can talk sometime after the wedding. If this is about my attempts to find Heaven on the streets, don't worry about it. I've been keeping myself busy at work. Lachelle cancelled my plans for a trip to South Carolina so I can focus on my cases here."

"I thought your supervisor was a male?" Mateo asked.

"Lachelle is my immediate supervisor. Her supervisor is a male," Rachel corrected him.

"Well, I don't think it's a good idea going into the roughest parts of town asking folks about Heaven."

"I agree and since my attempts have been unsuccessful, I'm resigned to letting the police do their job to find her. I'm not giving up, but it's a sad realization that there are so many children on the streets of the nation's capital city."

Before she disconnected the call, she instructed him to park his car in the tree lined circle in the front of her building and she'd come right out. However, he insisted on coming inside the building.

"I'm here." His voice over the speaker filled the front of her apartment and she pressed the button to unlock the security door.

"I'm coming down now." She buzzed him into the lobby where he awaited her arrival. After stepping one foot off the elevator, she stopped in her tracks. Mateo was leaning against the concierge's desk, swiping through his phone and chatting with Mrs. Luper. He looked dapper in a black tailored tuxedo, white shirt, dark red bowtie, and black shoes. His muscles were covered in a well fitted jacket, and if that wasn't enough of a sight for her to behold, he turned, giving her a full view of his dark eyes, jet-black silky hair tapered on the sides, and pearly white teeth. She wanted to reach out and touch his mustache and goatee, but her arms remained glued by her sides as she stepped toward him.

A well-dressed man in a suit always turned her on and Mateo wore his well. Her skin flushed as her body filled with unexpected heat beholding how at ease he seemed and the confidence that was ever-present. She had to focus on putting one foot in front of the other as her brain had short circuited and her legs were wobbly. Indeed, she was captivated by his rakish, debonair looks.

"Wow. You're handsome in that tux, my friend."

Mrs. Luper looked up and smiled but Mateo's eyes were big as saucers as he gave her a broad, toothy smile.

"You look beautiful," he said in that melodic tenor she had grown accustomed to hearing over the past week or so. He extended his arms and brought her in for a hug.

"Well thank you." She felt like a queen as he looked with such adoration and slowly twirled her for a full view of her half-shouldered crimson gown, accented with custom made bling, and matching stiletto heels.

"See you later, Mrs. Luper."

"The two of you make an attractive couple. Have fun at the wedding." She waved goodbye.

"Thank you, and it was nice to meet you, Mrs. Luper."

As a gentleman, he extended his arm and she placed hers in the crook of his elbow as he escorted her through the doors to his other vehicle, a black on black Lexus SUV. Unlocking the doors remotely, he assisted her into the passenger's side before hopping into the driver's seat.

The church was only about fifteen minutes from her home, and butterflies fluttered in her stomach as they wound their way through the city. Music always calmed her nerves and she tapped her feet to the Latin jazz playing through the speakers.

"Have you heard anything about Heaven." All week, he hadn't said anything about his investigation of her disappearance.

"Not yet, but we'll find her." He angled in her direction then turned his attention back to the road. Moments passed before he continued.

"There's something I wanted to talk about, but I thought I'd wait until we saw each other again. Do you still want to wait until after the wedding?"

"What's up? Might as well get it over with now."

"I've been worried about you all this week and I haven't hidden that from you."

Rachel nodded. "I know and I haven't gone back to those dangerous places looking for Heaven. I promised you I wouldn't, and I've kept my word." She crossed her heart, causing him to smile.

"Thank you. In my line of work, I specialize in keeping people safe."

Rachel was curious as to where this conversation was going, so she didn't respond.

"And you know that technology can be used in a myriad of ways, right?"

"I do." She stretched her legs out in front of her.

"Do you think there's a way you and I can agree that you need to be kept safe?"

Rachel looked at him, her arched eyebrow her only response.

"Okay, promise you won't say a word until I explain." Mateo rounded the corner, making a right turn at the traffic light.

"Okay," Rachel reluctantly agreed.

"Many people think that it's a movie thing, but there are items I can give you so if something happens, I can track you and get to you, ASAP."

She inhaled. "Mateo, I'll be fine. I made the mistake of keeping those darn earbuds in while I was running, and you know what I did to that dude."

"I do … which has me worried," he said. "What if they come up with a different plan, have reinforcements, or knock you out with something?"

Rachel hadn't thought about that. She knew she could defend herself against one attacker, but the thought that she may not be involved in a fair fight *next time* hadn't crossed her mind.

"I'll consider it." She knew he cared about her and didn't want to take his consideration of her safety for granted.

"Thank you. You know I brought up the subject and there's more to it, right?"

"I should've known." She sighed softly and waited for him to continue.

"There's something in the glove compartment for you. Open it."

She complied and found a little black box.

"What is it?" Her voice lightened as she tingled with excitement.

"Open it and see for yourself." His smile was irresistible.

Opening the box as if something might jump out at her, she paused and placed her right hand to her chest as she gasped at the sight of a pair of beautiful diamond earrings.

"I can't accept these...what...why?"

She searched for words and he held up his hand to stop her. She gave him the side eye, but was actually kicking herself for feeling a little disappointed that another piece of jewelry wasn't in the box.

"Pretty lady, these are a tracking device. You deserve more diamonds, and maybe we can have that discussion later, but for now the earrings will help to keep you safe and track your whereabouts."

"I see, and what made you so sure I need to be tracked?"

"I have a gut feeling about these things."

After a deep breath, she took them out of the box and exchanged them with the earrings she had on, then pulled the visor down to look at them in the mirror.

"I think we'd better be safe than sorry." He sighed, obviously relieved she didn't put up more of a fight about maintaining her privacy.

"So how do they work?" She put her attention back on his profile.

"It's very simple. To activate them, just pinch them with your fingers. like this." Mateo gave a light squeeze to Rachel's ear lobe, sending shivers down her spine.

"And the best thing is that if your hands aren't free, you can use your shoulder to activate them, as well. And remember, you don't have to activate both, one of them will work."

She turned her head admiring the earrings in the mirror. "The FBI has thought of everything."

"The bureau can't take credit for this invention. My friends who are into the latest security measures hooked us up with these."

"Tell them thank you." She looked out of the window along the drive. "We're almost at the church. What are you listening to?"

"Latin jazz."

"Do you mind if I search the stations?"

"Be my guest." He extended his hand toward the radio and turned to The Heat on Sirius XM. Glenn Jones' *I've Been Searching* blared through the speakers and she hummed along.

"So, you like R&B?" He turned up the volume. "That's a nineties jam, right there."

Glenn Jones' melody played while they both messed up the lyrics, but when the chorus came, they belted it out together.

Swaying from left to right and shoulders bobbing to the music, Rachel's reservations about coming to the wedding with Mateo dissipated. At first, she saw it as her friends's way of helping the relationship between them go a little faster rather than travel a natural progression. In hindsight, she realized it gave her another opportunity to get to know him better. Rachel had to admit she was growing fond of him and she wasn't adverse to dating someone outside of her culture. Since he had also grown up in Washington, DC, they still had a lot in common like listening to Go-Go music, particularly the legendary Chuck Brown.

"We're here." He placed his hand on hers before parking in a space close to the entrance. "Let me get your door for you."

He slid into his jacket before walking around to the passenger's side. Rachel placed her decorative wrap over her shoulders once the brisk breeze swept across her shoulders.

They arrived about fifteen minutes before the ceremony was scheduled to begin. Given Lachelle's penchant for punctuality, they had just enough time to settle in.

Rachel pulled the invitation from her crimson lined clutch.

"It says the ceremony will take place in the chapel behind the main sanctuary."

A few guests were walking toward the back of the cathedral facing a parking lot that looked as though it could hold hundreds of cars.

"Let's follow them. They might know where they're going." He gently laid his hand on the small of her back and a frisson of excitement surged up her spine.

As they rounded the corner, the entrance to a much smaller building came into view. A red carpet leading to the chapel was lined with ushers greeting guests and handing out cream and gold programs.

"Are you here for the bride or groom?" One of the ushers asked.

"Both." They looked at each other and laughed as the usher gave them a puzzled look.

"Rock, paper, scissors?" Mateo covered his right hand with his left.

"I don't believe you." She positioned her hands to mimic his and they hit their hands three times before revealing the results.

"I won," Rachel exclaimed in the narrow foyer.

"The bride's side, please," Mateo requested and they were seated in the company of an intimate number of guests.

"I guess we're high up on the food chain," he remarked and helped Rachel remove her cape.

"Lachelle told me that they weren't hosting a large gathering, but you're right. It looks like only about fifty people to me."

"And some recognizable faces, too."

Lachelle's attendants made their entrances. Adorned in burnt orange gowns with matching exotic flowers, they walked slowly down the aisle. A collective gasp filled the chapel when the doors opened to reveal Lachelle and her toddler daughter, Faith, who bounced and jumped down the aisle. Lachelle attempted to calm her, but she couldn't stifle Faith's unbridled joy.

Rachel almost melted when Lachelle and John presented their children with tokens of love exhibiting the blending of their family. Faith, two years old, didn't really understand the enormity of the occasion, so John's presentation was cute. He gave her a teddy bear which elicited a bright smile. But, when Lachelle presented John's twelve-year-old daughter, Hope, a bracelet with a gold heart-shaped charm, there wasn't a dry eye in the place. Rachel thought that was the highlight of the celebration...until they arrived at the reception.

John had retired from the NBA a few years ago. He wanted to give Lachelle an elaborate reception held at the world-renowned Skydome Restaurant. Located just six miles outside of the city on the fifteenth floor of the DoubleTree Hotel, it was a stone's throw from Reagan National Airport.

The valet parked their car and they took the elevators to the fifteenth floor. After receiving a table number, Rachel took in the stunning views of the DC skyline. Once Mateo returned to their table with their drinks, they enjoyed pointing out familiar national landmarks. The reception was enjoyed by all, and recognizable faces of those from the pro-sports and media community were in attendance mingling and consuming overflowing glasses of Moet and fancy hors d'oeuvres from waiters weaving through the mingling guests.

Rachel felt like a Disney princess hoping her evening wouldn't end. Would Mateo prove to be her prince charming? She looked at him and smiled as they danced together like they were the only two in the room enjoying choreographed movements of courtship on the polished wood floor. Or, was the truth of it that in her world, princesses were never saved by the gallant prince. They had to save themselves. She touched the earrings. Well, at least she had a way to be discovered if she was ever lost or in danger again.

Chapter Ten

"Do you want to come upstairs for a drink?"

They were in his car outside of her apartment building holding hands and listening to music.

"I'm having so much fun, I'm not sure I'm ready for this night to end. Thank you for being the perfect gentleman and making sure we had a great time."

She looked over and smiled as he seemed lost in his thoughts while Michael Jackson serenaded them with *Lady in My Life*.

"Is there something on your mind you want to talk about?" She placed her hand on his and he cupped it. Looking at her, she couldn't miss the concern in his eyes.

"Do you know how to shoot a gun?"

"Why, and where is that coming from?" She shifted her body toward his, and in her stockinged feet, she bent her left leg under her rear end.

"I can't shake this nagging feeling even though I know you're good with your hands."

He stroked his goatee and leaned back against his door, shifting toward her.

"I keep thinking that hand to hand combat may not be enough to keep you safe. Can you shoot a gun?"

"Actually, no. But I've always wanted to learn. Are you willing to teach me?"

"Suppose I told you that we could do it tonight?"

"Dressed like this?" Her eyes widened.

"I keep workout clothes in my trunk and instead of a drink I thought we could go upstairs and change into something comfortable."

She pondered his suggestion. "Are you serious?"

He nodded. "Yes, I am pretty lady."

"I'm down with it." She smiled and scrounged for the shoes she kicked off nearly fifteen minutes into the drive. Looking at the clock on the dashboard, a question came to mind.

"It's only nine-thirty, but where can we go?"

"I know people," Mateo replied as he grabbed his cell phone and swiped through it. "Let me call my main man who runs an arms training center. He stays open 'til close to midnight."

He connected with his homeboy, put in his request, and hit the *end call* icon on his steering wheel. "We're all set." He went to assist Rachel out of the car.

"It won't take me long to change." Excited that the evening would continue, she wrapped her arms around his neck and planted a kiss on his lips.

"Thanks for caring about me."

He leaned in and she positioned her head as he kissed her. Her blood heated with desire as his tongue caressed her warm and smooth lips, scintillating her senses as he explored the softness of her mouth.

"We'd better stick to the plan before we're distracted." He finally caught his breath as his chest heaved.

"So, I'm a distraction now?" Her arms were still around his neck.

"Only the best kind, Ms. Jordan."

He grabbed the bag containing his change of clothes and led her to the apartment.

* * *

Rachel tried to hold in her laugh but instead did her best impression of the seventies badass icon by holding her arm out as if she were about to shoot.

"I see you, Foxy Brown, but when we get to the range, I need you to focus."

Mateo was developing feelings for her and had not considered that being in close proximity to a woman who was so well put together and had all the qualities he wanted in a mate would cause him to let his guard down. She was not only a spontaneous, down to earth woman, but someone with class and style who could accompany him and hold her own. He had never met someone who could easily negotiate his personal and professional world.

She brought him out of his thoughts as he turned in response to her taps on his shoulder.

"Turn right." She pointed toward the GPS. "You just missed your turn. What were you thinking about?"

"My bad." He made a u-turn and then a left turn into an industrial park where they drove past Pump It Up Bounce Park and a FedEx building before pulling in front of the On-Target Firearms Academy. He parked and jogged around to assist her out of the car before walking hand in hand toward the front door of the building.

"Are you Mr. Lopez?"

"That's me."

"Mr. Rayford told me you were coming, and I reserved our most requested firing booth. He said nothing but the best for you. By the way, I'm Hector and I'll help you select your weapon and ammo." Standing at about five feet and nine inches with a mohawk haircut and curls spiraling out of his man bun, Hector gave them a welcoming smile.

Rachel remained close behind and he wasn't sure if she was excited or scared.

"How are you feeling? Do you still want to do this?"

"I'm fine and I'm so ready." Her eyes lit up and he was relieved.

"I'm glad I'm the person you're doing it with for the first time."

"Ahhhh, I see what you did there."

He shrugged and threw his hands up. "What?"

"You're the jokester and I like that. I'm glad you're my first too." She batted her lashes and gave him a coy smile.

"I like to keep things light. Come on over and let's pick out your weapon."

Hector was quietly typing an entry into the computer as they engaged in playful banter and after finishing his task, he looked at Rachel.

"Based on your size and stature, Ma'am, I'd recommend a Smith and Wesson .357." He walked toward a pad-locked glass cabinet, secured the revolver, and gave Rachel the weapon.

"What do you think?" She handed the weapon to Mateo.

"I think it's good, especially since it's your first time. This won't jam as some semi-automatics tend to do."

Hector nodded his approval. "It sounds as though you already know what you want, Mr. Lopez."

He slid a gaze to Rachel. "I sure do. I've got my own Glock .40 here, but will take some extra ammunition. We'll also take two sets of eye and ear protection."

Mateo carried both guns as they were led to a private booth. "Muy bueno, I like it."

Mateo had been to the facility before but only to shoot and had never taken anyone else or toured the place. But this time, Bill Rayford had hooked him up.

"This looks like the VIP room in a club," Rachel said as she laid her purse on the couch.

"Let me know if there is anything I can get you." Hector pointed to the buzzer. "We have snacks and soft drinks over there."

Mateo laid the guns and ammunition on the table then dug in his pocket and pulled out his wallet. "For your trouble." He extended his hand containing a large tip to Hector.

"Thank you, Mr. Lopez. You're too generous and I can't accept this."

"Yes, you can, for your excellent service."

Hector placed his hands together as if he were praying. "Thank you Sir."

"So, what's first?" She asked. "Do I watch you shoot?"

"First, we're going to go over some things. Both for the range here and in general."

Mateo went over a litany of safety rules and procedures, and then explained what all the different parts of the gun were and what they did.

Rachel laughed and said, "I thought this would be more exciting. I feel like there's going to be a pop quiz any minute."

Mateo became serious and as he held her eyes with his own, told Rachel safety was the most important thing, especially hers.

She felt that gaze all the way down to her toes.

She got a bottle of water and took a sip while she stepped back and watched Mateo prepare. He put on the shooting glasses and hearing protection, and extended his arms to shoot, while Rachel was reminded again of how amazing his arms, shoulders and back looked in his tight t-shirt.

"I feel like Angelina Jolie and Brad Pitt in the Mr. and Mrs. Smith movie."

"Trust me," he said. "Even they had to go through this training."

Standing in front of the mark, he explained everything he was doing and showed her how to insert the magazine into his Glock.

"I want you to watch me closely. Even though I'm a professional and I have a license to own a gun, I still have to attend training. I'm starting you off with a .357 because it's lighter, and you'll be able to handle the recoil when it fires."

"Recoil?"

"Yes, the gun will jump back a little. It's called a recoil or kick, and I don't want it to surprise you. Plus, it's going to be loud and the noise may make you jump."

She put on the ear protection and he fired his weapon at least ten times. Then he reeled in the paper target so they could gauge the results.

"Wow. You *are* good."

"Now, I want you to stand with your feet shoulder width apart, with your right leg slightly behind your left leg and keep your shoulders squared with the target."

She followed his instructions and waited as he went to get her gun.

Looking intently at the weapon, she took it and leaned back into him while he placed one hand on her shoulder to keep her balanced and steady.

Keep your cool Mateo.

She changed her stance and accidently rubbed against him causing a reaction he was ill prepared for.

"Are you comfortable? You keep fidgeting."

His pelvis tightened involuntarily, despite his attempts to remain loose and relaxed.

"I, umhh—"

She looked into his eyes then down at the bulge below his waist.

"Let me move my wallet." He quickly turned away to grab the wallet out of the front pocket of his pants and placed it in his back one while repositioning himself and waiting a few moments.

"Let's try it again." He put one hand on her shoulder again and helped focus on the sites and the target. His other hand rested lightly over the top of her wrist. He told her to gently squeeze the trigger.

Stay focused, man. Stay focused.

"One. Two. Three." She squeezed the trigger until she heard a loud bang and felt the gun raise up in her hand. She was excited she hit the target, although not very close to where she was aiming. Rachel jumped as she said, "oh my gosh! That was loud and powerful. She was so excited the gun started to stray from being pointed at the target.

"Give me the gun, Rachel. I don't want you to shoot me in the foot."

She complied and after he put it on the table, she fell into his arms.

"Mateo," she paused to catch her breath. "I didn't know how I'd feel when I fired my first shot, but that felt good…like really good." She relaxed and giggled which was music to his ears.

The icy wall around his heart hadn't been chipped at in a while. As a warm feeling settled in his chest, he realized he cared more about her than he probably should at this stage of the game. For the first time in a long time, he felt that his concerns for her made him vulnerable.

"Thank you." She turned and peered upward, and he studied her, hoping he was reading the message in her warm brown orbs correctly. He leaned down to meet her lips as she tilted her chin upward. This time they stayed connected to each other a little longer as their lips danced to a rhythm he hadn't experienced in a long time. He felt his passions stirring as the temperature in his body rose. His heart was beating out of his chest sending him a warning to stop. He needed to take his time with her and not take advantage of the fact that she had experienced many traumatic challenges over this past week. So, he pulled away and brushed his index finger across her chin.

"Why'd you stop?" She gazed at him and with a gentle hand, caressed his jawline.

"I didn't want to distract you," he replied as she pulled her ear protection to the side.

"You know you're yelling right?"

He removed his earmuff and then hers while smoothing her hair. His heart pounded as if driven to explode by the sensation of being so close to her. After wrapping her hands around his neck, she ran her fingers through his hair. Exploring below the crown of his head, down his neck, then caressing his chest, she stared into his eyes and drew him into a kiss filled with passion and longing.

"Dios Mio! Have mercy." He resisted the urge to explore under her shirt and stepped back. "Trust me. There's nothing more I'd like to do than move our relationship further along, but let's shoot a few more rounds first." He managed to communicate with bated breaths.

Rachel's raised eyebrow spoke volumes as she stared at him and smiled. "Oh, I'd like for our relationship to progress too, Teo."

"I could get used to you calling me Teo. That's how I'm known to my family and childhood friends." He rubbed her arms before assisting her with more firing practice until she was able to hit closer to the middle of the target's chest.

"Yes." Rachel did a fist pump and a little two-step move celebrating her improved accuracy.

She was beautiful and strong, and he didn't doubt the feelings stirring inside of him were genuine and not just lusting after her body. He was falling for Ms. Rachel Jordan, but first things first. They needed to uncover the mystery behind who wanted to hurt her. His desire to protect her was consuming his every waking moment.

* * *

They left the firing range and arrived at her apartment building close to midnight, but neither one was tired.

"Let me escort you upstairs."

"Sure thing."

Scanning their surroundings, they began walking along the path leading to the front entrance. With a sideways glance, he delighted at watching her hips sway.

They reached the front of the building and she pulled out the key fob when a rustling in the bushes snatched their attention.

"Did you hear that?" His hearing was heightened by the possibility of danger.

"It's probably a cat." She stepped to the side allowing him to open the door, but the rustling sound coming from the bushes grew louder.

"That's not a cat."

Mateo pulled out his weapon and stepped in front of Rachel to shield her with his body.

Chapter Eleven

"Who has my fifty grand?" Guy Brown didn't look up from his screen. After minimizing the open file on his laptop, he pulled out a stress ball from the top drawer of his black wooden desk. He preferred the scant décor in his office. With a few chairs scattered around the room and a leather black and white cowhide area rug, he was comfortable in the space that had no evidence of excess. Converting the warehouse into a makeshift boxing gym gave it the appearance of legality, and running his business was a priority. He often spent hours each day in the dimly lit office.

Jake Lowery often wondered why Guy chose this way of life. He could've been a preacher or anything other than a gangster. His charisma and intellect would've taken him far in life.

Ray Ray, Guy's first in command, had been with him from the beginning. They'd held each other down during their rough patches and enjoyed the champagne and bubbles when life was good. Prison was a given when you choose the drug game. They both did prison bids and could depend on each other to take care of their families when away serving jail time.

"You know the couple in Southeast that had the kids handling the business for 'em?" Jake hesitated before continuing. He knew the news wouldn't go over well. Business had been running smoothly, competitors kept their distance, and the block boys turned in their money on time. They had gotten so good at running their business, only infrequently did a problem arise. "I've spoken to someone that's on your payroll at the police station and the oldest girl wasn't there when they offed themselves. They said that the adults and two younger children were found, but no money. We think that the fifteen-year-old girl has the fifty grand on her."

"So, you're gonna have us out in these streets tracking down a teenager?" Guy zeroed in on Jake for emphasis. "That's not good for business."

Jake pulled one of the black chairs closer to the desk and sat down.

"Have a seat Jake," Guy snickered. They both knew that he allowed very few people in his world to explain a situation without first having an invitation for a meeting with him. Jake pulled out a pack of cigarettes, hit it against his hand, and pulled one out. Snatching a lighter from his pocket, he lit the tip of the cigarette.

"You plan on telling me today or what?" Impatient with Jake's delay, a look of disdain crept over Guy's face. "For your information Negro, second-hand smoke kills."

Jake didn't drink or do any drugs. Smoking was his only vice. "Really?" He shot back. "It's the only thing that I do that calms me. I'll stop on my birthday."

"You said that on your last birthday."

Jake inhaled and let out a puff of smoke before he began. "The Williams family had a good thing going with having those kids taking drugs to school. They also had an arrangement where they unknowingly sold to their teachers and other employees."

Guy fanned his hand back and forth to get the smoke out of his face. "But what happened?"

"They'd been fostering younger kids, those who wouldn't have a clue. But then this family had a fifteen-year-old and two younger brothers. It seems that she got wind of what was going on." He flicked the ash from his cigarette onto the floor. "The bottom line is that she wasn't even there when CPS showed up. I guess ol' dude thought they were gonna get caught." Jake shook his head in disgust. "That dude could've taken the rap."

Guy let out a strained, half laugh. "That dude wasn't built for jail. He did the best thing for us because he would've sang like Luther up in there." He paused and turned his head toward a sound coming from the door. "But we still have a problem that I want solved."

"I know, we'll find her and get your money back." The volume of Jake's voice rose.

Guy banged his fist on the desk. "Damn it, Jake. You have one job in this organization, and that's pairing kids with cooperative families… the right children."

Jake thought for a second before creating an elaborate lie to deflect blame. "Our CPS contact has been out for a week, otherwise we would've told Mr. Williams that they were coming."

Guy stood and snatched the cigarette from Jake's mouth. He snuffed it out on the back of Jake's hand. "Let me make this clear. Someone has my fifty thousand dollars. And the streets need to know that I'm the wrong person to steal from."

Jake winced before responding. "We'll get your money boss."

Guy sat on the edge of his desk. "She can't ID anyone can she?"

Jake shook his head. "The girl has never seen any of us."

This was the time to inform Guy that the case landed in the hands of his best worker. Common sense told him otherwise.

Jake knew what he had to do. In this game it was survival of the fittest and he was determined to survive.

Chapter Twelve

"Miss Rachel?"

She jumped and turned her head to the sound of the voice cloaked by the darkness and the lush bushes alongside the walkway. A dark figure came out with her hands up.

"Teo, put that gun away." Stepping in front of him, she pushed the weapon downward as she did a quick scan of the girl's features. "Heaven! Oh, my goodness. Come here. I was so worried about you."

Rachel pulled her in an embrace as Heaven grabbed her backpack.

"This is Heaven. The young lady who we've been looking for." Leaning back, Rachel gave the teen a full once-over. Although her hair was disheveled and her clothes were dirty, Heaven looked good for someone who had been living on the streets for over a week.

"Come on, let's get inside where it's safe and we can talk."

Mateo ushered them through the door and into the elevator. Rachel had never had anyone protect her before and she was grateful for his presence.

Once inside the apartment, Heaven looked around and plopped down on the leather sectional.

"I want to hear everything about where and what you've been doing over the past week."

"Okay Miss Rachel, but may I use your bathroom?"

"Sure, it's over there." She pointed to the closest one near her bedroom. "While you're freshening up, I'll fix you something to eat. Are you hungry?"

Heaven's eyes lit up and she nodded vigorously before heading to the bathroom.

"Teo, may I speak to you in the kitchen? I have some baked chicken, veggies, and rice in the fridge. After Heaven gets cleaned up, we'll let her eat… and then we'll talk."

He sighed, but nodded, itching to question Heaven. She told him she wanted to take care of the teenager's basic needs and offer her empathy following the loss of her siblings before they talked about anything else.

"I don't like this Rachel," he said peering out her front window. "A teenager finding out where you live and showing up unexpectedly means anyone else could find you if they wanted to, without much effort."

"Keep your voice down, Teo. What would you have me do? I'm not turning her away even though I also know she could have been followed. I'll go check on her and while I'm gone, can you pull the food out of the fridge?" She pointed to the meal after grabbing a bowl of sliced fruit.

"I'll also heat it," he trudged to the fridge as though reluctant to leave his post at the window.

"Thank you." She went to the hallway with a small bowl as Heaven was coming out of the bathroom.

"Let's go back to my room and I should be able to find something for you to wear. Here, I brought you a small appetizer while we warm up the food."

"Thank you." She grabbed the treats and stuffed them in her mouth. "May I take a warm shower? I haven't had one in a week."

"Of course." Rachel held out her hand to Heaven who took it but held tight to her backpack as they made their way down the hallway into her bedroom. Rachel closed the door behind them.

"You can have a seat right there." She noticed the fear in Heaven's eyes and motioned for her to sit on the settee beside the bed. "I'll get a towel, washcloth, and some clothes, then you can stay here with me for the night while we sort out the next steps."

A tear trickled down Heaven's face, and Rachel brushed it away before her chest began heaving with audible sobs. Sitting next to her, she embraced the teen in the same way that she wished someone would have done for her when she was first put in foster care. She learned to toughen up fast.

"Heaven, I'm guessing that you know what happened to your brothers."

She nodded and the sobbing onto Rachel's bare shoulder kept coming as if the weight of her grief would not let it come to an end.

"Let it out Heaven. I'm here for you." She continued to rock her.

"I didn't even get a chance to say goodbye."

"No sweetie, you didn't." Rachel responded.

"I blame myself for not protecting them. I'd left for school, but forgot my American History book, so I turned around. When I got back, the house was surrounded by cops, so I ran. I didn't know where else to go."

She looked up at Rachel and wiped her reddened eyes. "So, you're okay if I stay here tonight until I can figure out where else to go?"

Rachel held her even tighter knowing how it felt to be unwanted, abandoned, and tossed from home to home with a garbage bag for your belongings.

"We'll figure it out together. Let's get you cleaned up and we'll talk afterwards."

She found underwear with the tags still on them and some Juicy pink and purple sweat sets that were intended as Christmas gifts for one of her co-worker's daughters. She had purchased the wrong size and ended up buying a gift card at the last minute.

"I'll be in the kitchen and you can come out when you're ready."

She opened the bathroom door, but Heaven stood at the entrance, shaking and hesitant to go inside.

"Is there something wrong, sweetheart?" She placed a hand on her shoulder.

"Don't leave me. Please stay here while I bathe and then I can stay in the chair next to you. I promise I won't be a bother to you." She burst into tears and Rachel drew her in for a hug.

"Okay. I'm here." She pulled her phone out of her pocket and texted Mateo.

Rachel: I'll be in here for a while. Will you be okay staying in the living room until Heaven goes to sleep?"

Mateo: Her food is ready.

Rachel: Can you set it outside the door? She's afraid to be alone.

Mateo: Will do.

"How in the world did you know where I lived?" She asked as Heaven remained by the door.

"I saw your address on Felicia's pad when she came over to see us for the last home visit. I guess she was coming over here afterwards to get some food you prepared for a party she was having."

"Oh." She was relieved it wasn't the result of Heaven asking about her in the streets.

"Miss Rachel, sometimes I think I've lived in just about every neighborhood in this city." She slowly proceeded into the bathroom.

"I know and I think God purposely connected us through this journey. I didn't have it easy growing up. My mother kept me until I was ten years old when one of our neighbors reported her to Child Protective Services because she wasn't home. I was trying to cook dinner for myself one day and the apartment caught on fire."

"Did the building burn down?" Heaven's eyes widened as she gasped, and Rachel released a slight laugh.

"No," she answered. "I banged on the neighbor's door and she helped me put it out. It scared me to death. Ms. Wilcox had enough of my mother neglecting me and called Child Protective Services."

"At least you were an only child," Heaven mused, looking down at her hands. "I tried to look after my brothers and messed that up."

"Hey, hey. You loved them and did your best to look after the three of you. Remember you are a child and children aren't supposed to take care of other children."

Heaven absorbed Rachel's words for a few moments.

"Did they have a funeral? Did I miss that?" She looked up at Rachel who hesitated in answering her question.

"Take your shower and let me get your food."

"Okay but promise me you won't leave this room."

"I won't, and I'll talk to Mr. Mateo at the door."

She finally convinced Heaven to go into the bathroom by leaving the door ajar. She wasn't sure how Heaven would take the additional news about her siblings. When she opened the door to signal to Mateo about the change in plans, she found the tray he had left with a small vase containing a flower with the flair of a gourmet presentation. The food was placed under a dome to keep it warm. A bottle of lemonade and a glass containing ice were placed on the tray. He even wrapped the cutlery in a colored napkin that was left over from the luncheon she had prepared for her coworkers. Her mouth dropped as she overheard him humming as he stacked the dishwasher.

He's a keeper, sensitive, and sexy as hell. I think I've hit the boyfriend lottery.

Chapter Thirteen

After Heaven's shower, Rachel placed the tray in front of her, sensing there was a shift in Heaven's mood.

"Sweetheart, I need to tell you that there was a small memorial service and your brothers were cremated."

Chewing her first bites of food, Heaven looked up from her plate. "Do we know where their ashes are?" Her eyes moistened, but no tears fell.

"I don't right now, but we can find out." Rachel was concerned as Heaven gave her a blank stare, rubbed her eyes, and rested her chin in her left hand.

She has to be in a state of denial and shutting down her emotions. This child may not be able to handle the weight of this situation.

Aware of how devastating grief could be, Rachel was determined Heaven would not have to face it alone.

"Okay Miss Rachel. Anything else?"

"Try to eat something."

"I can talk and eat." She looked up at Rachel. "I mean…that's not rude?"

"No, it's not."

"I know that you want me to explain some things." Heaven picked up her fork.

"I do, but only when you're ready," Rachel assured her.

After stabbing the fork into the chicken, chewing it as though it would be her last meal, Heaven responded, "I'm ready. I knew that I had to find you because I have lots to tell you."

Heaven poured some of the strawberry lemonade into the glass over ice before she continued. "I've been on the street and there are a lot of teens living out there, but they helped me find food, and a place to lay my head. Most of them ran away from home and created a new family."

Heaven stopped and gulped down her drink. "I really thought I might find my brothers and I kept praying, but then I overheard a conversation in a warehouse where some of the kids go to get out of the rain or the cold. I knew I couldn't stay there long, because I didn't want to get caught up in the things I saw some of them doing to survive."

"What did you overhear?"

"Two men talking about our so-called foster parents and my brothers. They said that they were glad that they did what they did because Mr. Williams wouldn't be able to make it in jail. They—"

Rachel saw the despair and sadness settle in her eyes. Since she didn't want her to feel like she was being interrogated, she was supportive of her taking her time.

"I know it's hard, but just remember I'm here for you," Rachel whispered, stroking Heaven's arm. "You don't ever have to worry about being alone again and you can share anything with me."

"They want what's in my backpack." She patted the bag.

"There's a lot of money in there. They said something about fifty thousand dollars."

"Why do you have the money, Heaven?"

"I took it from the drug dealers."

Rachel shut her eyes tight as her heart sank into the pit of her stomach hoping somehow this wasn't true. She had been around long enough to know the code of the streets, and she knew the drug dealers would stop at nothing to get it back. They wouldn't risk having anyone else find out a fifteen-year-old had stolen money from them and could identify them. She sighed, recognizing that despite the serious consequences of Heaven's actions, what was done was done. She didn't want to scare her, so she opened her eyes and tried to remain calm.

"We'll solve this problem with Mr. Mateo's help. He's a professional who's on our side and he'll know what to do to keep you safe."

"I should've left the money in the warehouse, but," Heaven was silent for a few moments before she continued speaking. "I *wanted* them to be mad." She made a fist and frowned. "I want them to miss something like I'm missing my brothers. I know nothing can bring them back. The money doesn't compare to what I lost…what Caleb and Justice lost. We're not the only three that they've hurt. They use other foster kids to sell their drugs for them."

"Do you mind if Mr. Mateo comes in here and you tell us how it worked?"

"No, please Miss Rachel, I don't know if I can trust him right now." Her gaze darted about the room before she placed her hand out to stop Rachel from leaving.

"Alright, we can talk to him later." She gestured to the half-eaten meal. "Finish your food."

"I can tell you about it. I trust you." Heaven scooped up a portion of the rice with her fork before continuing. "Ma Williams would put the drugs in my backpack and someone at the school would put money in there and take the drugs. When I got home, they'd take the money out, but I never saw this large amount of money before and I'm not sure what it was for."

"Interesting." Rachel tilted her head upward pondering what the purpose for so much money was, but she also wanted to get more information on the other children that Heaven had seen in the warehouse. "Did you get a chance to find out where the other children came from or if the drug dealers had them doing anything?" Heaven washed down her mouthful of chicken with a sip of lemonade.

"Oh yeah. I know that they did things that they didn't want to do. We'd see some of them getting paid to go into different rooms with men and I'm talking girls and boys, too. Some stood in front of stores and sold drugs. Those guys have a lot going on in that warehouse. They use kids and they know they need to eat and have a place to sleep. I talked to some of the kids and the warehouse was better than where they came from, so they went along with the program."

Heaven was bright but she wasn't telling Rachel anything she didn't already know. She was sad that Heaven, or any other child for that matter, had to come into contact with the evil side of the world at such an early age. They had their innocence stolen. Like blinders snatched off their faces, they get to see all the ugliness around them.

Her phone vibrated in her back pocket and she pulled it out and read Mateo's text.

"Sweetheart, Mr. Mateo needs to speak with me, but I'm not going anywhere. I'm just going to let him out and lock up the house. I'll take your tray." She placed it on the desk beside the bed and stroked Heaven's hair before covering her with a soft fleece purple blanket accenting her lilac queen bedspread.

"I promise you," she whispered. "I'll be right back."

She left the room with the tray and closed the door gently behind her. Mateo was waiting for her on the couch and she placed the tray on the table.

"Do you think I should stay here with you tonight? I could sleep right here." He yawned, patting the cushion beside him and stretched.

"I think we'll be fine." Letting out a long sigh, she plopped on the couch.

"What else did she tell you?"

"A lot." Rachel gave a full account of Heaven's conversation. "Those guys have kids out here, knowingly and unknowingly selling drugs for them. She also mentioned sex trafficking or prostitution in some warehouse."

Mateo's eyes grew dark as they narrowed. "If it's the same warehouse I'm thinking about, we shut it down years ago."

"You never know. It could be new people, but the same game."

"You might have a point," he said. "I can begin talking to some of my associates and have them track down these fools."

He drew her nearer and she placed her head on his shoulder.

"We had a nice time this evening, but I want you to go home, get some rest, and we'll connect tomorrow. Heaven doesn't feel comfortable having you here and I know she has trust issues, especially with men."

She felt his desire to protect her as he wrapped her in his strong arms. It felt good and she wanted to stay there forever, but she had to put Heaven first.

"I could get more information if I stayed tonight. Did she tell you where this warehouse is?" Mateo placed his chin on top of Rachel's head and held her close.

"She was kind of vague which warehouse it was because she said they only went in and out at night and there were a ton of warehouses in the area."

"It's probably off of New York Avenue. I'll get a few men together and we can start there first."

"And that would make sense because it's not too far from here." She nodded. "Okay, I need to get back to her and she's probably wondering what's taking me so long." They both stood and faced each other with lingering gazes.

"Rachel, I'm thinking I should stay tonight. I have a gnawing feeling about leaving you and Heaven here alone."

She pulled back and touched the side of his face. "We'll be fine, Teo. You don't have to worry. Besides, Heaven and I have each other."

He sighed in resignation. "Don't leave this house for anything tonight. You hear me?"

"Yes, sir I do, and I won't."

He extended his strong biceps, wrapping his arms around her waist, and the heat from their sexual chemistry radiating from him to her almost took her out.

"Alright Mr. Lopez, it's time you get on your way," she said the words signaling her intent that they stick to the plan for him to leave, but she was slow to pull away from his strong hands resting on her hips.

"Come on, let me get you out of here." Grabbing his hand, she led him to the door, while he looked at her like a big puppy that had lost his best friend.

"I'm leaving, but remember what I said."

"Yes, sir." She stood at attention, bringing her right hand to her forehead, with her palm faced downward, saluting him.

"You got jokes for one beautiful woman." He planted a sensual kiss on her lips and stepped back. "I'm talking about on the inside as well as physical beauty."

"Thank you and I'd better open this door before something gets started that neither of us will want to stop."

"Yes, I guess it's good we have a chaperone." He smiled and cupped her face in his hands.

"A very good thing. Goodbye, Teo."

"Promise you'll call if you're concerned about anything. No time is too late." He focused his attention and narrowed his eyes.

"I promise." She crossed her heart and smiled.

"Good night, Rachel."

They kissed one last time before she opened the door, watched him walk to the waiting elevator, and waved as he got on. Closing the door, she was careful to check the top and bottom locks, and even pulled the door to ensure that it was closed tightly before walking away.

"Darn." She remembered that in her haste to get ready for the wedding, she hadn't completed her laundry and had left a few towels drying in the laundry room which was only a few feet from her apartment. Hesitant at first about retrieving the towels, she decided maybe it was best not to leave.

The leasing office fined people for keeping items in the dryer over two hours after the cycle completed and had posted a recent reminder in their newsletter.

She frowned and went back to the bedroom where she found Heaven sitting in the chair, her eyes laser focused on the door.

"It's just me. I need to walk out to the laundry room to get a few things from the dryer. You can stand at the door and watch me. I won't leave your sight."

"Okay."

They walked back to the front of the apartment and Rachel smiled at Heaven as she pointed to the laundry room.

"I'm going right in there to get my towels. Lock the door and stay here. I'll knock and let you know it's me, alright?"

"Okay."

She entered the hall and waited for the sound of the locks turning before proceeding to the room.

Pushing the door open, she reached for lights on the left side of the wall and felt a strong jerk sending searing pain up her arm. Pulled into the darkened space, she resisted as a cloth was placed over her mouth. Slowly, her eyelids descended as she faded to black.

Chapter Fourteen

Awakened from a light sleep by his phone vibrating, Mateo peered at the clock in the darkened room and the red numbers on the face of it informed him it was only five forty-five in the morning. The call on the phone from *unknown* almost went to voicemail, but he thought about Rachel and swiped the phone from the nightstand, pressing the flashing green button.

"Who is it?" He yawned and blinked as he tried to focus on the caller.

"I have someone who would like to say something to you," a deep baritone voice came across the speaker.

"Mateo! It's me and Hea—" He jumped up hearing Rachel's voice screaming in the background.

"I think you've heard enough to know that we've got your girlfriend and the kid too and we don't want nothing except our fifty grand, within the next forty-eight hours."

He paced before heading to the bathroom. "I'll get you your money."

"Remember forty-eight hours or you won't recognize them when you see them again," the menacing voice threatened.

"If you know what's good for you, you won't touch a hair on their heads."

"Just do what we say, and we won't have any problems."

"Let me speak to—"

The call ended abruptly, and he went to his contacts and found Dro's name.

He answered on the first ring.

"Dro, I know you're an hour behind and it's super early, but I've got a problem."

"Slow down, Teo. What's going on?"

He shifted the phone from one ear to the other and took a deep breath.

"I just received a call from a kidnapper who has Rachel and the little girl that we've been looking for. And they want fifty grand." He rubbed his hands along the side of his face while he continued to pace his bedroom.

"The money is the least of our worries. That's on the low side and I've got that and then some."

"I left her alone, Dro. I should've stayed with her." He slammed a fist against his forehead.

"Teo, I need you to focus," Dro said. "Were you able to get that tracker on her?"

Dro was right. He couldn't help Rachel if he didn't calm down and give him as much information as he could.

"Yes, she had them on when I saw her last night."

Dro sighed. "Then we're off to a good start. I'll jump on the first thing smoking to DC."

"They told me that we have forty-eight hours to get them their money," Mateo told him.

"Mi hermano, trust me. You'll see Rachel and the little girl in less than a day. I don't let my brothers down."

He could no longer deny his feelings for Rachel, and he'd do whatever he had to do to get her back.

His heart pounded in his ears as fear that this man would do something to hurt them threatened to overwhelm and paralyze him. With every beat of his heart, his blood raged through his veins, and he vowed he would exact retribution upon those who snatched her. He tightened his fists and fought to banish the images from his mind of someone threatening or hurting the woman he loved.

Is she tied up or gagged?

This wasn't supposed to happen to someone whose sole purpose in life was to help others.

"Teo?" Dro's voice turned his attention away from his darkening thoughts.

"I'm still here. What do you want me to do?"

"Nothing but be available by the phone and I'll let you know when we land in DC."

"Do you need any surveillance equipment or information on the city?" He let out an exasperated sigh.

"No, The Kings come with our own set-up and your living room will be used assurveillance central. We got you."

"Okay, See you soon."

* * *

Mateo had Carlos do a sweep of Rachel's apartment and struggled with the idea of going over there himself. He realized what Dro advised him to do was sound advice and stayed available by phone. He wasn't comfortable with the thought of doing absolutely nothing and he recalled the names of some folks he'd met during his undercover days who might be able to tell him about the warehouse Heaven mentioned. The information would be useful in getting Rachel and Heaven out safely.

He also knew there was no honor among thieves, nor did gangsters do what they said they'd do. Giving them the fifty thousand dollars wasn't a guarantee he'd see Rachel again. As he warred with himself about getting others in the Bureau involved, especially after the sting in which several agents were discovered working for the cartel, he eventually decided against it and focused on Dro's promise that The Kings would help him find Rachel.

His chest expanded as he reflected on Rachel: her smile, her strength, her beauty, and her caring spirit. He couldn't deny that she was an amazing woman as he recited one of the shortest prayers he'd ever prayed in his life, "God, let them live. Bring her back to me."

Chapter Fifteen

Rachel recalled the timeline in her head from hearing dripping water when she woke up until now. She tried to move her hands forward, but they were tied tightly behind her back. The pain from jerking against the ropes caused her to wince. Her anxious breathing calmed as she turned her head to the sound of a familiar voice.

"Miss Rachel. Miss Rachel," Heaven whispered. "I've been trying to wake you. Someone took us from your apartment and brought us here." She could understand how they got to her, but how had they taken Heaven?

"I tried to fight them after I saw them dragging you into the elevator," Heaven told her as if she was reading her thoughts.

"I told you to stay in the apartment." Rachel groaned as pain seared through her head.

"I couldn't let them take you. I just couldn't." Heaven blew out a breath. "I stepped into the hall and I didn't think the door would slam shut and lock me out. I had no choice but to fight for you and me."

"I understand." She closed her eyes. "We need to focus on getting out of here."

The room was dark without any markers of the time of day. Tears threatened to fall, but she found solace in remembering Mateo's strong voice laced with the sound of guilt. She should have listened and stayed in the apartment. She had to hold on to hope that her decision to leave the apartment despite her promise to him, wouldn't cost her and Heaven their lives.

Sitting on the cold hard ground, the two of them were bound together back to back and they used each other as a back rest.

"Did you recognize the man who called Mr. Mateo?" She whispered.

"No, I didn't. But, while you were still knocked out, I heard someone call a man named Jake. But that's all I heard." Heaven twisted her fingers intertwining them with Rachel's. "My pants are wet, I think I peed on myself."

"Sweetheart, the fact that we're here and alive is a blessing and that's natural. We'll get out of here. Mateo will make sure of that."

"I wish there were windows in here so we could see. There could be rats running around." Heaven tried pulling her legs closer to her chest.

Why did she have to say that?

Rachel wondered why they weren't gagged. Maybe no one was around; so screaming and yelling wouldn't matter. She had to get them out of here.

"How are you feeling? Are you okay?"

"Miss Rachel, I'm scared and hungry. But I think I'm okay. My legs are weak and feel like they have pins sticking them."

"They've fallen asleep because our blood isn't circulating." Rachel tried to shift her hands around and a pain, she could only describe as a migraine, pounded against her right temple causing her to lower her head.

Moments later, she saw a light coming from her right side and heard a door creaking followed by footsteps entering the space. The light soon disappeared.

"We haven't heard back from your boyfriend yet. Do you think he even cares about you?" A sinister voice sneered, piercing the darkness and frightening Rachel, but she was determined he would not see her fear.

"Did you try to kidnap me last week while I was out jogging?"

"Maybe so, maybe not." He stood above them lighting a cigarette as she tried to get a view of his face; the glow from the cigarette didn't illuminate it as much as she hoped. Instead, she focused on the distinct sound of his voice. He pulled out his phone which gave off more light.

"Are two lives really worth fifty thousand dollars to you?"

Their captor moved around the room and Rachel followed the light from the cigarette and from the glow of light from his phone.

"You know the game. We don't know how much you know or what that kid has told you about our enterprise. If you had only done your job and minded your business, you wouldn't be here."

"You're scum…making money off kids," her voice spat. "It's people like you who I try to keep away from children."

"But you didn't this time, did you?" He snarled and his pungent breath assaulted her nose.

That voice.

Rachel heard Heaven's sobs and felt her back moving up and down with each cry. A heaviness settled in her chest as she became aware of the identity of this man and what he planned to do to them. She knew in her spirit that he didn't plan to let them go once he got his money.

I do know the game, unfortunately.

She had grown up in this city during the time when DC was the murder capital of the nation. If someone was believed to be a snitch, they were as good as dead.

"Don't you have a mother?" She asked. "Maybe you have a daughter, and would you want someone taking advantage of your loved ones?"

Rachel tried keeping their captor preoccupied with small talk while they loosened the knots in the rope holding them together. Using the dark to their advantage, she hoped he couldn't see what was going on behind their backs.

"My family members know how to listen, and I don't have a runaway daughter." His voice agitated Rachel's headache, but she needed to continue to engage him and get as much information as she could.

"You don't know the horrors they're running away from while you and your crew prey upon them, luring them with false promises of things they've only imagined in their dreams. I can only *pray* for your soul."

"Shut up," he roared. "Don't come up in here talking about God. Ain't no God and if there was one, do you think he'd come in here to save you?"

Rachel tried to focus on the place in the room she last saw. "I do believe that with every fiber of my being."

His deep anger rang through Rachel's ears. As she twisted her fingers, she raised her shoulder to the earrings to trigger it, praying it would lead to their rescue.

Activated by a renewed hope of being found, she knew she still had to do everything she could to free herself. She twisted the ropes and kept working to loosen the knots.

"Try not to get too comfortable, ladies. I'll come back with the boss man when he's done handling some business. Peace out."

She had the confirmation she needed, and she now knew without a doubt why her captor's voice was familiar even though he tried to disguise it by speaking a few octaves higher.

Rachel had seen him every day for the past two years. Those two words were Jake Lowery's favorite way to exit a room.

Chapter Sixteen

Daron Kincaid, Dro's brother King, arrived in DC after receiving Mateo's call. Daron's specialty was all things tech and he was the king of their organization who was responsible for the tracking device Rachel wore. Originally developed to help women and children who had been stolen due to sex trafficking, he used his technical skills and passion to protect women and was in his element.

Mateo's living room was now surveillance central, as the silver suitcases Dro and Daron brought concealed high-tech touch screen monitors that were now strategically placed around the room. It was four o'clock in the afternoon according to the clock on the mantel. Over ten hours since he last spoke to Rachel. Mateo paced the length of the living room and watched them complete their set-up.

"Is there anything I can do?" He pulled a chair from the corner, moving closer to the desk and plopped down next to Dro who shook his head and kept his attention on the console.

"Does she know how to use the earrings?" Daron inquired.

"She had them on when I left her, and we discussed them at length."

Daron glanced at Dro and then back at Mateo. "I hope she didn't take them off before leaving the apartment."

"We'll know in a minute if the device has been activated." Daron advised as Mateo watched him plug in more equipment then he looked back at Mateo.

"Do you have an extension cord?"

Mateo's jaw dropped in disbelief; a high-tech genius needing an extension cord?

"And let me get your Wi-Fi code, too."

He trotted over to his hall closet and rummaged through a few boxes before pulling out three extension cords. The Wi-Fi code was etched in his memory and he gave it to Daron.

Time moved slowly, but Daron remained cool without any sign of panic as he watched the gadgets light up in various colors.

"When the earrings are activated, I'll receive a ping. As long as she's in the same place for a least an hour, we can track her. If they're moving them from place to place, it will make it harder, but if we're dealing with street thugs, those thoughts won't cross their minds."

The minutes crept by until a flashing green dot appeared on the touch screen monitor and Mateo leaned down to get a closer look while Daron pressed his fingers near the flashing dot, pinching them and spreading them apart to zoom in on the screen.

"What does that mean?" Mateo's nerves firing sent electric sensations down his arms and he ran his hands through his hair.

"I've got their location on lock, at least within a one-mile radius and according to this. The earrings are tracking here and let's hope that's where Rachel and Heaven are too." Daron pointed to the location on the screen.

"The street names are there?" Mateo squinted to get a better look.

"Are you familiar with New York Avenue, Mateo?" Daron asked. "It looks like it's in the Northwest quadrant of the city."

"It's considered the warehouse district, some of the buildings are used, and some are empty."

"Apparently some are supposed to be empty but used for illegal purposes." Dro scanned in on his monitor. "How far is it from here?"

"DC is small. It's no more than a ten-minute car ride."

Daron's eyes narrowed and his body was still. "We need to develop an escape plan and get them out before those fools decide to move them."

Dro glanced up from his monitor, directing his question to Mateo. "Do you have any connections who can help with intel on the area, or who might be able to give a layout of the land once we determine which warehouse they might be in?"

Mateo reached for his phone on the table, hit the screen to wake it up and scrolled through his contacts. Carlos had been integral in taking down a drug crew in that area a few years ago. He provided information to them on video feed. Although they worked in different areas of law enforcement, Mateo knew Carlos was the best in his field. He also contacted Roger Woods, a fellow FBI agent he could trust. Roger wasn't as big as Mateo, but he stood at a solid six feet tall with a lean, muscular body like a National Football League running back. They could use all the muscle they could get.

He also used his designated street phone to call trusted contacts, including a man he only knew by the name Eric. These folks had come through for him in the past when he worked undercover.

Mateo understood the importance of a street team and his brother's words rang through his mind, 'keep it in your back pocket'. Without hesitation he scrolled through his contacts and found Juan's number. Juan answered on the first ring.

Mateo drew in a long breath, "Mi hermano, I'm pulling out that favor."

* * *

"Roger will bring the layouts that he has within the hour. Carlos, along with my street contacts, will meet us at the Ivy City Smokehouse to fill us in on what they know."

Although Daron kept his eyes glued to the screen, he inquired about Rachel.

"Mateo, Dro filled me in, as much as he could, while we were on the plane. He told me that she can defend herself."

"She can. And that's what has me worried the most." Mateo stretched his legs out in front of him and leaned back in his chair. "She's quick on her feet so I know they took her by surprise, probably grabbed her from behind. I just taught her how to use a gun. So, we can add that to our fire power, as well."

"Do you think she'd use a gun to defend herself?"

Mateo thought back to the satisfaction she felt firing her weapon and how well she mastered the gun at the shooting range. "I believe she would, and I think she'd shoot to kill to protect herself or someone she loved."

* * *

They reviewed the layout of the warehouses in the Ivy City section of DC with Roger. He brought about eighty percent of the printed plans for the warehouses in the area within thirty minutes after he was called. Since the warehouses were all built at the same time in the late sixties, the layouts were practically identical. Carlos gave them additional information from a recent DEA bust in that area.

Mateo treasured the relationships he'd established as an agent. He'd met some dudes who were in the game at one time but had turned their lives around and now held down nine-to-five jobs. Although his one-time partner at the Bureau wasn't as honorable as he thought, he knew many agents whom he could trust with such a sensitive undertaking. Roger was one of them. Today these bonds would pay off for him by helping him find the woman who had unexpectedly stolen his heart.

Moonlight filtered through the blinds, casting a glow across the dark hardwood floors in his living room. They returned to execute their plan and could've been called the men in black with their black pants and black polo style cotton shirts.

Daron provided information on the technology part of the plan. "I'll stay here and monitor the tracking system."

Daron opened a suitcase Mateo hadn't seen used before, a smaller version of the large silver ones they had trudged into his house. Mateo looked over Daron's shoulder as he pulled out several things including two outfits that looked like personal protective equipment and a few small devices.

"Take these." He held out his hand to Dro who immediately placed the device in his ear.

"It's a listening device," Dro said, turning his attention to Mateo who followed suit by placing the tiny device in his ear. "You'll be able to hear me, but I won't be able to hear you. You'll need an additional piece of equipment that will allow me to hear what's going on."

"What's up with the safety suits? They look like hazardous material suits." Mateo asked Daron.

"They're sort of like that. I call them 'Emperor's Suits,' a device that fools the naked eye and causes the person wearing it to appear camouflaged and blended into the environment."

Daron held up the suit to ensure Mateo's suit would be a good fit before giving one to him and Dro. He then presented them a wire that was much more sophisticated than anything the federal government had ever provided their agents, much smaller and sleeker.

"I'll want to see what's going on, too." He gave them both a pair of glasses to wear.

"If these become cumbersome or if you're in a tight spot, just slide them in your pocket. They're nice to have, but it's not necessary."

"Y'all came with the thunder, I see." Mateo tilted his head, impressed by their operation as Dro raised his shirt, and kept his arms in the air. Daron attached the other device in the middle of his chest.

"I told you brother; we handle our business. Unfortunately, you're seeing it for the first time and dealing with the situation of getting your lady back safe and sound. We'll talk more afterwards because it would be nice to have a knight here in DC."

Mateo complied as Daron signaled him to raise his arms. "I could see myself working with brothers who have a passion to clean up the inner cities that are so often plagued with crime." He nodded. "Could I roll with you all and also have my own security company?"

"That's the plan," Dro agreed while Mateo thought he would give it more consideration. First things first, he had to find Rachel and Heaven.

"We're ready. Let's roll." His connection was waiting for him at the entrance of an alley about five hundred feet from the Smokehouse.

Dro remained in the car while Mateo talked to Eric, but he never let Mateo out of his sight. Once they finished talking, Mateo jogged back to the car and hopped into the SUV.

"Just as I thought. The Ivy City Crew used to run drugs and women through these corridors a few years back and was disbanded when their leader got arrested. He plead guilty to lesser charges and got out of jail about six months ago. It sounds like he's started the enterprise up again. This time, he's added a twist with a connection in the foster care system. The game is that they connect foster parents who use the children for the monthly check and recruit those parents to sell drugs for them using the children any way they can. They don't care if it's through the school system, the street corners, and other family members."

Dro scanned the area directly in front of them. "This is their base?"

"Eric thinks we should focus on warehouse number 323."

As Mateo pushed the button to start the car, both men put their hands on their weapons, cautious as a black Ford Expedition pulled up beside them and the window rolled down.

"You didn't think we'd let you do this alone did you? We always roll with El Gato." Roger and Carlos gave him a head nod.

"Mi hermanos. Brothers forever." Mateo fought back the emotions of pride and gratitude settling in his chest, and breathed a little lighter knowing he had all the men he trusted the most joining him in this raid.

Laughter rang out as a throng of millennials spilled out of the Smokehouse and the two cars screeched away from the curb, making a U-turn toward the warehouses. Daron's voice blared through their earpieces. "I've got an exact location."

Chapter Seventeen

"Jake, is that you?"

"What if it is?" He growled in his normal voice and revealed his face.

"I knew I recognized that voice."

He let out an evil chuckle and bent down close enough for Rachel to smell his malodorous breath. She turned her head to avoid the stench.

"I told you to leave the case alone. But you just wouldn't listen." Through gritted teeth, he hissed. "Why do these kids mean so much to you? They may cost you your life."

Rachel activated the tracking device again the moment he moved away from her.

"I should've let the boss man sell this sweet little thing on the market. We could've gotten a load of money for her."

Out of the corner of her eye, she saw Heaven recoil as Jake stroked her hair and though her jaw was tightly clenched, she roared like a mama bear. "Don't touch her, you…you pedophile. I should've known something was wrong with you, always wanting to take the cases with young girls. I can't wait to see you locked up, right along with your crew. I hope you never see the light of day."

"Who's going to catch me, Boo?" He taunted her in a feminine voice. "Certainly not you. We should put you up for sale too, but nobody would want your old rusty tail." He leaned forward again and laughed.

"You are really a sick puppy." She was defiant and tried to calm Heaven's sobs by rubbing her hand. "Using your job to assist criminals to hurt children. You do know what they do to pedophiles in jail, right? I know you do."

"Stop calling me a pedophile," he screeched. "I haven't touched those kids." His face was so close to Rachel's, she could almost taste the Mexican food he had for lunch.

"But it's the same thing. You're responsible for what happens to them. You knew they were running kids in and out of this place."

"Shut up," he yelled. "The only thing you need to worry about is Mr. Brown getting his money; or else you're dead, both of you. But trust and believe this, I'll be long gone before anyone finds you since I plan to take a family visit to Cuba. I think it'll be a nice place to retire."

At that point, Rachel felt the ropes loosen a little more. "Can someone bring us some water?"

Jake rose and a threat spilled from his lips. "Maybe. I guess it's the least we can do before we dispose of your bodies."

Heaven's cry rang throughout the space as the sounds of his footsteps became more distant.

"I need you to be quiet, Heaven." She calmed down once they heard the door open and close, as Rachel struggled with the rope again.

"Can you loosen it?"

"Yes. It's not as tight as it was before." Heaven's voice was steady.

"Were you pretending to be upset a few minutes ago?" Rachel asked.

"I thought it's what he'd expect."

"Good girl. Once we get out of here, we'll have to put you in some acting classes." The rope loosened and fell to the ground. "See if you can find something we can use as a weapon."

They crawled around and Rachel's right hand landed upon something cold, hard and metallic. Lifting it closer to her face, she examined it.

"I found a crowbar. Hurry, let's get back to where we were sitting."

They scurried back to the spot. Rachel sat on the crowbar before they assumed the position they'd been in for almost twenty-four hours. Rachel touched her earring with her hand once more for good measure, then placed her hands behind her back, clasping them with Heaven's.

"You'll know when I'm going to make my move because I'll squeeze your hand three times. After the third squeeze, I'll grab the crowbar and hit him in the head with it."

The door squeaked open and Rachel's adrenaline kicked in, putting her in hyperalert mode as Jake's footsteps came closer. She breathed in and out waiting for Jake to come within reach, hopefully with his hands full. She stroked Heaven's palms, a silent reassurance that they would overtake him and escape.

Jake returned with two white Styrofoam cups and just as he looked down to set one of the cups on the cement...

One. Two. Three.

Rachel extended her right leg, grabbed the crowbar, and with every ounce of strength, came down on Jake's head with a vengeance. He fell back and hit the concrete with a loud thud.

"Run!" Rachel tried to keep her voice low but firm. Heaven raced to the door and Rachel hit him again, this time in the kneecap, hearing a loud crack before making a break for it herself. They slowly cracked the door open, peering out carefully prior to venturing into the dimly lit hallway.

"Stay close." Rachel glanced at Heaven over her shoulder.

Scurrying down the hallway, they came to a stop as they approached an office and stood outside the door. She prayed no one would sneak up behind them as they listened to the conversation involving one criminal telling the other how they planned to explain to the boss why they had to kill two men they believed were from a rival gang.

"I don't think he's going to be mad. After we get rid of the women, we can tell him. What's two more dead bodies?" They shared a chuckle.

Rachel knew they were as good as dead if they were captured, but there was no way past the office without being spotted. As she made the choice to turn around and try the other direction, they heard another set of voices ahead of them.

Think.

Her heart threatened to come out of her chest as she scanned for a safe place. Spotting a utility closet across the hall, she gestured to Heaven to make a dash for it.

They jammed themselves inside and discovered an uncovered hole on the side of the wall that may have been an old airduct. Heaven pointed to the opening as sweat plastered their shirts to their bodies despite the cold temperature in the warehouse.

"We're going to climb through there to wherever it leads." Rachel quietly pulled a box from the corner. "Stand on this. I'll help you up and it'll probably be tight, but if it's a duct, we should make it through." Heaven stuck her head into the opening.

"It looks like it leads somewhere."

"Great. On three, I'll give you a big push."

She hoisted Heaven into the hole and then jumped up into the space with Heaven's help. Once inside the duct encased in the darkness, Rachel took the lead and moved as fast as she could, crawling on her stomach, over the weak rusted, crumbling metal. They reached the end of the large cylinder covered with a collection of heavy dust, thick debris, and old shredded filters blocking their escape.

"I can't see anything." She placed her hand to her mouth to muffle her cough. "There's a lot of dust and old filters ahead of us. I'll see if I can clear the path." She moved forward in haste. As Rachel bent her arm and pushed her fist to the other side, she stifled a scream as she hit her elbow against a hard structure covered by the debris. Suddenly, the top of the duct began to cave in, covering her in dust.

"Go back." She waved frantically urging Heaven to retreat as she heard cracks forming in the bottom of the duct before it crumbled. Her arms flailed as she fell through the foundation that disappeared beneath her.

Chapter Eighteen

"Do you see anything?" Daron asked through the device in Mateo's ear while Dro, Roger, and Carlos guarded the entrance of the shaft for the ductwork they had located as the best way to enter the warehouse undetected.

Mateo readjusted the glasses so he felt comfortable with them on.

"Even though I have visual capabilities as long as you wear the glasses, we'll need to talk to each other constantly ... of course to the extent that you can," Dro emphasized. "It'll pick up a whisper so don't feel like you need to talk loud," Daron's voice came through the earpiece instructing him. "I'll be able to hear a mouse peeing on cotton while you're in there."

"Okay, I understand." Mateo responded to Daron.

Roger clapped his hand on Mateo's shoulder as he stood beside Dro. "Don't take any unnecessary risks, buddy. I wish you'd let at least one of us go in and find them. I'm concerned that you're too close to the case."

Mateo still felt a tinge of guilt for leaving Rachel and Heaven in the apartment alone last night when he knew better. He should have insisted on staying. He didn't want to leave it up to anyone else to get her out of this predicament. If something went wrong under someone else's retrieval, he'd never forgive himself. With so much on the line, he needed to do this for himself and for Rachel.

"I'm highly trained for this. When Rachel sees me, she'll know which direction to run in. I don't want her confused trying to determine who you are and if you're a friend or foe." He peeled off his lightweight jacket, tossed it into the front seat of the car and pulled a pair of black leather gloves over his fingers.

"I'm ready." Mateo clenched his fists and gave each man a double fist bump before returning to the side of the warehouse and entering the narrow space. Roger furrowed his brow as Mateo hit his chest with his right hand three times to reassure him, he was manned-up and ready for the challenge.

"El Gato lives." He reminded Roger who gave him a nod of support. The last sound Mateo heard was the siren of a police car and he bent down, remaining motionless until the sound grew distant. He wondered if the space had the dimensions needed for his muscular frame to crawl the length of it. According to the layout they reviewed, he should be able to maneuver it without difficulty.

"What do you see?" Daron communicated with him after he had progressed several feet.
"Nothing," he whispered back. "It's very dark in here and I don't know if there's something ahead blocking my path."

"My tracker says that you're on level with Rachel. Right now, you're facing south and within five hundred feet you're coming up on a dead-end so you'll have to turn left or right entering another portion of the duct work." Daron instructed Mateo. "I'll need you to go right and then keep going north. That's when you should end up closer to her. I see your tracker and hers. It's moving…looks like through the old duct system but not at a quick pace. I'd bet she has escaped and found her way into the ducts. That might be a problem if the duct you're in can't hold your weight and hers."

"That's my girl." Mateo smiled and picked up the pace. He knew she had skills, but he was worried someone could be on her tracks. "I've passed the entrance now."

"Good. You have a little over five hundred feet, maybe closer to six. There does seem to be something blocking your path. Do you think you can clear it? It's probably just debris."

"I see it up ahead. I'll try to move it out of the way."

"Looks like Rachel's tracker is getting closer to you! Clear it quickly if you can. I don't know what's behind it." Daron's voice blared through the earpiece.

Mateo crawled in front of the blockage and drew back his fist punching through the shredded filters with small pieces of metal running through it. Luckily, it didn't fly off like a dangerous projectile. Only a piece of it fell to the side before he punched again and more fell out allowing him to look through the hole he had created.

"Rachel!"

"Mateo." He eased his body forward and pulled her toward him. "I'll get you out of here." He brushed away the debris on her face and pressed his cheek to hers. "Is anyone on your trail?"

"No, but we've got to go back and get Heaven." She held him tightly. "I fell through a hole in the duct above us a short distance from here. I told her I would go get help."

"Don't worry. We'll rescue her." The fear in her eyes and her shallow breathing moved him to kiss and reassure her. "I've got Rachel and I'm going back to get Heaven," he notified Daron.

"We've got this babe. It's going to be alright."

From his experience in these situations, if she or Heaven panicked, it would make it harder to get out.

"I knew you'd come." She hugged him. "I knew it."

"Of course, I would." He crawled back through the duct in front of Rachel and came to the gaping hole where he found Heaven staring down at him, her eyes pleading with him to save her too. He didn't want to risk the duct caving in if he added Heaven's weight too quickly.

"Grab my hand." Mateo's voice was steady and slow as he swallowed the lump in his throat.

Heaven tried grabbing his hands, but he couldn't reach her.

"Teo, please save her," Rachel cried.

"Heaven look at me. I'm gonna climb on top of the duct and reach for you. Lower your body as far as you can without falling into me then I will slowly pull you down. Do you understand?"

She nodded. The duct started making creaking sounds and Mateo looked down at the cracks forming under the added stress of his weight combined with Rachel's. He turned back to Rachel and then focused on Heaven who was a few inches shorter.

He raised his body and extended his legs, anchoring them to the walls of the duct.

"We've got to move quickly." He gritted his teeth.

"Come between my legs and keep them pushed apart." He urged Rachel as she complied, steadying herself on her stomach. Turning his attention back to Heaven, he saw the tears forming that refused to fall.

"I need you to slowly inch toward me." He instructed Heaven, who was wide-eyed with fear.

"On the count of three, stretch as much as you can and grab for me. Understand?"

She nodded and leaned down into the space below her.

"One, two, three," and in one fluid movement, he scooped Heaven from the duct above him.

"I've got her, Rachel." She crawled back. "The cracks are getting bigger. Move backwards before we all fall through." He groaned and struggled to push backwards while pulling Heaven out of imminent danger.

"Let's get out of here." Pieces of the foundation fell as they moved back toward the exit. Mateo's heart raced as he heard echoes of pieces of rotted metal falling below them.

"What's that noise?" An angry voice coming from below caused their adrenaline to kick in as they scrambled as fast as they could.

"They're getting away. Lock all the doors." The footsteps of those running to carry out the order drummed in Mateo's ears.

"That's Jake," Rachel alerted Mateo as she crawled behind him.

"You know him?"

"Yes, but it's a long story."

"Yo, Mateo, try to get a move on it," Daron warned. "I'm seeing some serious activity close to you."

"Copy that."

After crawling a few more feet he found the entrance and passed it so the women could exit before him. With help from Dro and Roger, they were assured that they wouldn't fall onto the rocky pavement and hurt themselves.

"Got you." Mateo heard Dro's voice as he pulled Rachel out of the space. When he doubled back, making his way to the entrance, he saw Heaven's legs moving at a rapid pace.

Roger grabbed Rachel, who had Heaven's hand, and ushered them to his Ford Expedition as they heard the roar of Harleys, speeding toward them.

Rachel gazed over her shoulder before Roger shoved her into the SUV and locked eyes with Mateo.

"Go! Get them out of here." Mateo tapped the back of the SUV twice. Roger's tires screeched against the gravel before hitting the pavement, traveling east onto New York Avenue. He hoped Dro served as decoy, so they'd attract the two motorcycles toward them.

"Are you ready?" Dro placed a hand over his gun tucked away in the back of his pants.

"I stay on ready." Mateo wasn't sure if Dro heard him or not as the roar of the engines came closer to his SUV.

The motorcycles stopped short, causing dirt to fly through the air. Neither Dro nor Mateo lost eye contact with the drivers but kept their hands in place so that their company would know this wasn't a game.

The men jumped off their motorcycles and one lunged at Mateo and the other went after Dro. The larger of the two ran toward Mateo throwing a right jab. Mateo ducked, causing the attacker to lose his balance as he threw a punch, hitting his attacker directly in the eye. Following his initial blow, he landed a two-piece counterattack hit to the ribs, then to his stomach. Mateo stunned his attacker who fell to his knees, holding his side. Crying out in pain, the man rolled on the ground coughing up blood.

Dro's assailant was no match for him either. He turned, lifted his leg, and drove a sidekick in the thug's chest causing him to stagger backwards. He tried to rush at Dro once again who met him with a round-house kick knocking him off his feet. He landed on his face unconscious.

As Mateo walked toward Dro, the other thug bum-rushed him from behind. While they were on the ground, a fist slammed into his jaw before his head hit the gravel. He recovered, quickly jumping to his feet as they circled each other.

Smiling, he welcomed the few seconds to regain his bearing before his attacker lunged at him. He grabbed his arm and slammed him to the ground.

"Come on Teo," Dro yelled as the door to the warehouse opened and a gang of men spilled out. A bullet shot through the air. Dro ducked, fired back, and assisted Mateo to their truck. He looked over his shoulder as Carlos came from around the other side of the warehouse with a swarm of DEA agents.

"Get out of here. We got this," Carlos yelled to Mateo as he and the other agents returned fire. Dro jumped into the driver's seat and sped off after Mateo scrambled to the passenger side.

"I need to get you to a hospital. You took a hard fall and you might have a concussion."

"I'm not going to the hospital." Mateo leaned against the headrest after he entered his home address into the GPS. "Just take me home. I want to see Rachel."

Mateo wiped his face with the back of his hand thinking his nose was congested only to find blood on the back of the glove. He opened the compartment between the two seats and pulled out several napkins from various fast-food restaurants.

"They're fine. They made it here safely," Daron spoke to him for the first time in a while.

Thoughts raced through Mateo's mind, not about himself, but for Rachel's and Heaven's safety.

Mateo needed her alive, but someone still wanted her dead.

Chapter Nineteen

Rachel ran to the door as Daron, responding to a noise outside, shielded her before he opened it for them to enter. Taking in the panoramic beauty of the city from Mateo's home, high up on a hill, she reflected on the stark contrasts in the city. The white light of the Capital sitting to the left of her view was illuminated against the darkness of the night. The ugly side, or the underbelly, that she'd come to know firsthand, was at odds with the more visible, well-known side that most people travelled every day welcoming the tourists who viewed monuments proclaiming liberty and the pursuit of happiness. The throngs of government workers who helped to keep the city and federal agencies running, and the major businesses that thrived on the lighter, storied side of the city covered sinister happenings just beneath the surface.

A black SUV rolled into the driveway and Mateo stumbled out of the car. As he walked toward her, Rachel saw he had been injured.

"You're my knight, Teo." She helped him into the house and enveloped him in a heartfelt embrace. "Mi Angelito, my guardian angel." Speaking the message of her heart, she gazed at him with admiration as she caressed the side of his face.

"You're hurt." Placing her arms around his waist, she led him to the couch and fluffed up the pillows behind him for added comfort.

"Wait, where's Heaven?" He squeezed his eyes shut and rubbed his forehead.

"She's resting in one of your guest rooms," she responded. She looked down at him and stroked his arm. "I'm really concerned about you, Teo."

"Not to worry. The room spun around a little, that's all."

"I'm glad you can joke about this. But we need to get you to a doctor." Her fingers tenderly explored the back of his head, finding a small knot.

"I don't need a doctor," he said in a low husky tone. "What I need is to make sure you're alright."

Dro was the first to intervene. "Bro, you may have a concussion."

He tried to laugh but groaned in pain. "Look. I've had concussions before and if I have one now, I'd know it."

She laid his head against a pillow then took a seat on the couch next to him, unwilling to let go of his hand.

"You're quite the funny guy, I see." Dro frowned and went to the table where Daron was seated while Mateo turned and smiled as Rachel caressed his hand.

"I think we need to unpack what Rachel found out while they were in the warehouse." Mateo noted.

Rachel nodded, "I have a lot to tell you about who's involved and what they've been doing."

"Wait, where are my manners? I need to formally introduce you to everyone. Dro and Daron, this is Rachel. My—" He blushed as there was an awkward silence before Rachel laughed and introduced herself.

"I'm Mateo's friend."

Dro stared at both of them and chuckled. "So, Mateo is out here risking his life for a friend? Y'all are hugged up like you can't get enough of each other and that's what you're telling yourselves right now?"

"You heard what the lady said." Mateo peered at Dro. "So, tell us what you know Rachel."

She explained about the drug and sex trafficking exploits that were going on at the warehouse. "Once they take the kids off the streets, they can't go anyplace else. They're accompanied by someone at all times who threaten and coerce them into the life of a sex slave."

"Weak, despicable men always take advantage of the most vulnerable." Dro shifted in his seat as he voiced his frustration.

She sighed and continued sharing her thoughts. "The thing that hit me the hardest and what scares me the most is that I discovered my supervisor, Jake, is involved."

"That's how these operations typically work. A reputable person with access to people who are easily led astray, gains their trust," Dro added and shared a look at Mateo. "He or she sends them down a dark and narrow road that often leads to their destruction."

"Jake who?" Mateo asked. "I knew someone named Jake back in the day. And I mean way back, like right out of high school."

"Jake Lowery," Rachel responded, stroking Mateo's right hand.

He sat quietly with a blank expression despite hearing the buzz of Dro's cell phone.

After pulling it off the table in front of him, Dro glanced at the screen. "I need to take this in private."

Mateo extended his arm and pointed to the left. "Those stairs lead to the basement."

Dro put his phone up to his ear and mouthed, "thank you," before turning and scrambling down the steps.

"Hey." She tapped Mateo on the shoulder. "Do you recognize the name?"

"Unfortunately, I do. I used to run with a Jake Lowery doing stuff that lost young men in their teens do in this city. We tried our hand at hooking up with the drug guy who controlled the territory in our neighborhood. I learned it wasn't worth it. Evidently, he didn't." Mateo shifted his body on the leather couch and groaned.

"I had no idea that you and Jake knew each other." She relaxed her head on the back of the couch.

"We don't anymore. I haven't laid eyes on him since the day I walked away from that game." Mateo grimaced again.

"Can you take your shirt off?" She asked and he complied, pulling at the tail of his shirt. "If you won't let a doctor examine you, I want to give you a once over and clean your cuts." She marveled at all the tattoos exposed on his arms and chest.

"I'll go get my first aid kit." Daron left them alone.

"Wow, you have a lot of tats. I've heard they can be painful." She examined him with her fingers, touching the artwork on his arms and chest.

"Some of them were." He turned and looked at her, grabbing her hand a little tighter before he continued speaking.

"You will find out sooner than later, so I'll tell you the rest of my story now. I was in a fire during an FBI operation gone wrong and a so-called partner wanted me dead. It was unbelievable what happened. I almost died." He closed his eyes tight and bit down on his lower lip before he continued.

"I was in a relationship at that time, and my lady was trapped in our home when a bomb meant for me went off. I rushed into the house and pulled her out, but she died of smoke inhalation. I received a bad burn on my left arm trying to save her. My first tattoo covered up the burn, then one turned to two, then three, and you can see that I didn't stop."

She ran her finger along the outline of one of his tats, touching it lightly, and then another. "Do they mean anything in particular?"

"They represent the Mexican gods; fire, peace, and the spirit of the culture."

"I like them, especially the tattoo of the jaguar."

"Hmm, most people think it's a leopard."

"If they knew you, they would know you have the warrior spirit of a jaguar; humble and patient yet strong, powerful and confidant."

"Thank you, Rachel." Embarrassed by her assessment, his cheeks and neck reddened, as he spoke barely above a whisper.

"Can I ask you something?" Using her index and middle fingers, she followed the outline of the tats on his chest, tentative about what she was about to ask.

"Sure, you can ask me anything."

"Do you still think of her, the love you lost?" She bit her lower lip and waited for his answer.

"I've grieved her loss if that's what you're asking, and I'm ready to love again."

Lowering her head, she placed it on his chest, and wrapped her arms around his waist. Dro returned to the living room. "Sorry for the interruption, but I put in a call to Jaidev Maharaj, one of our brother Kings. He operates the Chetan Health Center and specializes in the connection between physical, mental, and spiritual healing. He's contacted one of his partners, Dr. Woodson, who operates a similar center here in DC."

Rachel lifted her head and turned to listen to Dro.

"I reached out to him after you told me about the kidnapping, and I thought Rachel and Heaven might be able to benefit from treatment to cope with their traumatic experiences."

Mateo gave Dro a side-eye gaze.

"He's world-renowned," Daron added, returning with a basin of water and his first aid kit.

"Talk therapy, acupuncture, aromatherapy and warm stone massages, that's the type of therapy he provides. He's made arrangements for the ladies to have medical personnel on-call as long as we deem necessary."

Dro looked at Mateo as he spoke. "Jai happens to be in town for a conference and he said we can bring all of you in, first thing in the morning. He'll meet us there and make the formal introduction to his colleagues."

Rachel couldn't believe the extent these men protected and cared for women as their mission and passion. Her headache from earlier today eased as she relaxed. She wondered what a difference meeting men like these when she was younger would have meant to the course of her love life. Would she have had all the trust issues and difficulties with intimacy?

"I believe we should seek help. Heaven and I need to rid ourselves of the energy from that place. But I'd like to talk to her first, and we can have you examined, Teo," Rachel told him. "I understand. She's been through a lot," Dro chugged down the last drop of his bottled water. "Daron and I can clean up this stubborn man while you check on Heaven."

"Teo, please listen to them." She kissed him on the lips before leaving to find out if Heaven was awake. After reaching the room at the end of the hall, she knocked on the door.

Who is it?" Heaven sat up as Rachel stuck her head in the door.

"Can I come in?"

"Yes. I was hoping it was you." A relieved look washed over the teenager's face.

Rachel reminded herself Heaven didn't trust any of the males in the house and was probably uncomfortable outside of her presence.

"Of course, it was me. I wouldn't leave without telling you. We're in this together, remember." Rachel came across the room and settled onto the twin bed across from Heaven's.
She smiled at Heaven. "Mr. Daron and Mr. Dro have offered to help us get some assistance … a little healing because of what we went through."

"I'm okay." Heaven shrugged, and lowered her gaze on her lap. "Heaven, no one who is kidnapped is all right. Trust me, we should get some help to deal with the trauma we've been through, or it can affect the way we interact with people for a long time. I'm going to be honest with you, I am not okay."

Heaven yawned and shot Rachel a look of indifference.

"I know you're tired and I am too. So, why don't you get a few hours of sleep and we can talk more about it in the morning."

"Okay." Rachel was surprised Heaven didn't resist.

"I'm glad there are two beds in here. Are you okay with me sleeping in here with you?" Rachel smoothed out the covering on top of the bed.

"I think it's a good idea. Maybe I'll get more sleep if you're close. I tossed and turned before you knocked," Heaven confided.

"Then good, it's settled." She smiled but found it difficult to cut through the indifference Heaven wrapped around her as an emotional safety blanket. She understood Heaven needed to be treated and probably had post-traumatic stress disorder as a result of the abuse, disappointments, losses, shame and fear she had suffered in her short life. She didn't even know where she would be living next, but Rachel resolved to give her some stability.

"Heaven, maybe if I share a few things with you, it will put your mind at ease."

"What is it?" She shifted to one side, propping her head with her elbow resting on the bed and gave Rachel her undivided attention.

This was the first sign of interest she had seen in Heaven since she entered the room.

"You and I," Rachel used an index finger to point to Heaven and then at herself, "we've been through a lot together. I want you to know that I'd like to do what I can to become a permanent part of your life."

"You mean adopt me?" Heaven's eyes lit up and she sat up on the bed.

The gleam in her eyes melted Rachel's heart as she reached across the space between their beds and held out her hand. "If you'll have me."

Heaven joined Rachel on her bed and wrapped her arms around her. "That would be dope."

"I think we'll make a good team. We'll get you into a school where you can focus, and there'll be one more thing that I believe we should do. We really should go to therapy together. Not too many people can relate to what you and I have experienced as children and I'm still suffering from the effects of being bounced from house to house. Until an angel, my last foster mother took me in and loved me." Rachel shared. "Are you okay with that?"

"And you'll be with me?"

"Right by your side."

Rachel and Heaven talked a little more before Heaven began yawning again.

"Are you going to be alright if I go back out and check on Mr. Mateo?"

"You just want another kiss." Heaven teased. "I'll be fine if you leave the lights on. I like Mr. Mateo and I know he likes you too." She giggled, and the sound warmed her heart.

"I think he likes both of us," Rachel said, cupping Heaven's face in her hands. "There's one last thing I want to say to you before I go into the other room. You are not a foster child; you're currently in the foster care system, but you're first and foremost a child of the most-high God who doesn't have a foster anything."

Heaven absorbed the words for a moment. Tears welled up and spilled down her cheek. She wiped them away with the back of her hand.

"Miss Rachel, do you go to church?"

She paused before answering. "I do, but I don't participate as a member as much as I used to."

"I'd like to go to church, too. I've never been, but I pray. I think God must've heard me and answered my prayers because he brought me to you."

Rachel's heart opened. "I think he answered mine too."

"One thing before you leave. Do you think they'll let you adopt me?" Her forehead creased with worry. "I mean, do they let caseworkers adopt foster kids? I mean kids in the foster care system."

Rachel knew it wasn't something that happened often and Heaven needed transparency. This had to be the foundation of their relationship and she wanted it to be strong.

"Not often," Rachel replied, "but there are no rules stating it can't happen. Once family court finds out everything that has happened, I believe the system will support us one hundred percent."

She hoped she had answered Heaven truthfully. Unfortunately, that very same system had a broken foundation and seldom did the right thing for those who needed it the most.

"Good night, Heaven." She said. "I'll be in the living room if you need me."

"Good night, Miss Rachel."

Stopping in the bathroom before she took the short walk down the hall, she gathered a sheet, a few washcloths, and soaked them in a basin she found underneath the cabinet in warm, soapy water then grabbed a small bottle of essential oils.

"Is he asleep?" She whispered to Dro and noticed Teo stirring.

"He took a little rest after Jai swung by for a quick moment to look at him. He gave him nothing stronger than an over the counter tablet for the pain. He's been resting quietly since then, but we had to keep him from checking on you."

"Is Jai the doctor you told us about?" She stopped at his desk and placed the basin on the table in front of the couch.

"Yes, he wanted to make sure Mateo didn't need anything more than a bedside examination. He was disoriented at the time and Jai recommended that he get rest."

Looking back at him, she smiled as he yawned and blinked his eyes. "Hola, sleepy head."

"Hola but, I wasn't sleeping. How is Heaven?" Mateo answered as Dro looked at him.

"I'm going to leave the two of you together while I get some rest," Dro told them. "We have a team in the neighborhood so, don't worry, we're on it."

"Gracias, mi hermano." He smiled at Dro and attempted to rise but stopped to put a hand to his head and closed his eyes.

"Teo, please rest and I'll show Dro out." She placed her hand on his shoulder and guided him so that he was flat on the couch before she rose to escort Dro.

"I'll see myself out, Rachel. Take care of the hardheaded one over there. At least, he listens to you."

"I'll do my best." She smiled at Dro and turned to Mateo with furrowed brows and a look that said she wasn't playing with him tonight.

"Alright, I'll be good. Adios, Dro."

She waited until the door closed and the click of the automatic lock went into place. Just outside the window, men in black were triggering the security lights as they walked by on their watch.

"They are guys from my company and from The Castle. We're safe with them all out there."

"I'm not worried." She turned and twisted the washcloths, wringing out the excess water before she applied it to his head.

"Daron did a good job cleaning your wounds."

Scanning his face and torso, her gaze landed on a four by four bandage that had been applied to his right arm. Most of the dirt and grime on his body from earlier combat efforts were gone.

"How do you feel?" He glanced at her face and then focused on her hands as she applied the warmed cloth to his face.

"Better, now that you and Heaven are here and safe with me." Closing his eyes, a small smile lifted the corners of his lips. She watched as he savored the water and the smell of the soap on his face. Gently, she cleansed his forehead, cheeks, and sealed it with a kiss. She grimaced from the pain in her side as she leaned over him. His eyes were still closed so he didn't notice she was still sore from trauma during the kidnapping.

"You'll sleep better after I finish your sponge bath. Your doctor ordered that you rest."

She continued cleaning his toned, muscular chest and he watched intently as she focused on her task.

"Yes, Nurse Rachel." His chuckle was infectious, music to her ears, followed by a boyish grin spreading across his face as she lifted his arms and washed under them.

"Ticklish, are we?" She dipped the cloth back in the water before caressing his chest with her hands and the cloth.

"I'll deny it if you tell anyone." His face warmed.

Her hands descended to the waistband of his pajama bottom and he quickly grabbed the sheet to cover himself.

"I apologize if I'm embarrassing you, but I can't hide that I'm attracted to you and—"

She placed a finger to his lips. "There's no need to apologize Teo. We're both grown, with healthy adult needs."

"It's more than lust for me, Rachel. I don't see us as just casual acquaintances."

"I don't think there's anything casual about our relationship either and I knew it the first time I laid eyes on you." She gazed at him and then finished cleaning his chest.

"The same thing is true for me. Once this is over, and it will be, I don't see us just going our separate ways."

"Are you saying you want a relationship with me?" Her heart warmed at the thought that he could also see a future for all of them.

He touched her hand. "Yes, I do."

"Well, right now, I need my man to rest and I don't want to take advantage of you when you're temporarily disabled."

"Do you promise to take advantage of your man in the near future?" He raised an eyebrow in a fashion she found endearing.

"That's a promise I plan to keep, but we'll both know when the time is right to take our relationship to the next step."

"Thank you, Rachel, for taking care of me." He didn't say anything further as she raised the hem of his pajamas and washed his feet and massaged them with oil. Silently focused on her task, she kept her eyes low as he bent his arm and covered his eyes.

"You've been a blessing to me, Mateo Lopez."

"Same here babe. You can't imagine how much you have blessed my life."

Chapter Twenty

Rachel and Heaven slept until ten in the morning. The smell of bacon drew them out of their beds.

Mateo knocked before saying, "Breakfast is here. I had your clothes laundered. They're outside the door."

"Thank you." Rachel called out from behind the closed bedroom door. They'd worn the same things over the past few days; they were grateful Mateo had their clothes laundered overnight while they dressed in his old night shirts and robes.

Once they showered and dressed, they entered the dining area, where they were greeted with orange juice, waffles, grits, eggs, and bacon.

"This looks delicious," Rachel said as Mateo pulled her chair out and then assisted Heaven, who seemed surprised by his gesture. Yes. She definitely needed to witness this on a regular basis. "Are you feeling alright?"

"The headache is gone, and I thought you would appreciate getting today started with a big meal, so I ordered everything on the breakfast menu from the restaurant nearby." Mateo dressed the table and served the food family style as he wasn't sure what they liked from the variety of food he had ordered. He said grace for the table.

"Why are those two SUVs pulling up in front of your house?" She asked before putting a spoonful of grits in her mouth. All three of them looked outside and noticed the trucks parking in the front yard.

"Oh, a security detail has been assigned to you and Heaven now that I'm working with the Kings. Until we bring down Jake and the people he's dealing with, we need to keep you safe. The plan is to strike now before anyone gets away, so we have eyes on all the major modes of transportation out of the city along with a surveillance of Jake's house. I'm not taking any more chances and I won't have the two of you vulnerable to another attack."

"I appreciate your concern, I really do, but I have to go home to get some fresh clothes and I want to take Heaven out to get some new things."

"Thank you, Miss Rachel, but I don't want you to spend money on me."

"It's not a problem," she added addressing Heaven's concern before turning her attention back to Mateo.

"Like I was saying, we have a lot to do today. Our appointment with Dr. Woodson is at one o'clock and—"

"Slow down, pretty lady. You know I've thought about all of that." He took a seat next to her at the table. "Remember, I told you about my company, Global Security Connections? Well, some of the guys outside have worked for me on some of my contracts; protecting the mayor and other notable people when they come in the city. They know how to guard without being intrusive."

He understood she was an independent woman and didn't want her freedom taken away, but there wouldn't be a freedom to be had if she wasn't still above ground. As he looked at Heaven chewing her bacon quietly, a sly smile appeared and then he turned to Rachel.

"Remember, I did ask you to stay in your apartment and not leave?" He took a bite of his toast.

"Now that felt like a stab in my heart." Rachel feigned death and fell back in her seat, but he wasn't laughing.

"So, we're good?" He placed a hand over hers. "You'll listen to them because they're only here to ensure your safety." He raised an eyebrow, waiting for her response.

"I will."

Heaven nodded as Mateo grabbed their hands and squeezed them as he spoke directly to Heaven. "I understand the last few days have been a whirlwind and you've been through a lot. What I'm trying to say is that I'm here to help you and Miss Rachel. The men who are helping me are on our side and they won't hurt you or Miss Rachel."

She looked down at their joined hands and up at his face.

"Since Miss Rachel trusts you," she said, "I trust you. I've been watching you Mr. Mateo. I've learned you can tell who to trust by looking deeply into their eyes, and your eyes don't lie."

His eyebrow shot up after hearing her assessment. "Are you sure you're only fifteen years old?"

She paused and leaned in to look directly into his eyes. "Yes, and even though I'm fifteen, Miss Rachel said she wanted to adopt me."

"I think that's a good idea," Mateo smiled and gave her hand a gentle pat. "I've been watching the two of you also. I think the two of you work well together."

Squinting, she narrowed her eyes and tilted her head.

"He's telling the truth, Miss Rachel. I see it in his eyes."

He hadn't let himself think about having a family for a long time. With all the time Rachel spent looking for Heaven in dangerous places, and how broken up she was following the memorial service for Caleb and Justice, he wasn't surprised now that the two of them were a package deal. And it didn't bother him at all. He thought that the demands of his career had stolen his future and dreams of having a family, but watching Rachel and Heaven enjoy breakfast in his home gave him renewed hope that maybe there was a chance of him becoming a part of the package too.

"Your protection is a Godsend, and I'm sure I speak for Heaven too when I say thank you. I promise I will listen and I'm sure we can work something out." Rachel let out a long slow breath.

"Can I go back to my, I mean your room, Mr. Mateo? I'm still sleepy."

"Sure. You've had enough to eat?" He smiled as she pulled away from the table.

"I'm good. It's been a long time since I've had a meal like that." She patted her stomach and left them sitting at the table.

"I'd better clear the table and do the dishes." Rachel rose, but he stopped her.

"Leave them for later. I would love the pleasure of your company in the living room."

He took her hand and led her to the soft leather sectional where he eased onto the cushion and sat with his arms around her.

"A warm, safe place to stay, breakfast, and now I'm in your strong arms. I'm beginning to believe you're courting me Mr. Lopez." She caressed his bicep.

"Believe it." He couldn't hold back the smile on his face.

"Touché, Mr. Lopez. I couldn't have said it better." He leaned in for a quick kiss and looked at the clock on the wall.

"It's getting close to eleven o'clock and I don't want to be blamed for making you late."

"I'm excited about our first healing session today." He lightly touched her nose with his index finger as she smiled. "I've never had this type of outpouring of support in my life. But what keeps tugging at my heartstrings is how this support will help Heaven to heal."

"It will be good for both of you," he added as she rested her head on his chest. Neither said a word for a few minutes until the clock's bell echoed in the background.

Mateo whispered, "It's time. Let's do this."

* * *

After gathering their few things, he escorted Rachel and Heaven outside towards the SUVs. Their security detail formed a protective shield around them as they climbed into the luxury vehicles.

"Aren't you coming with us?" She leaned over the guard after he closed the door, leaving Mateo standing in the driveway.

"No, I'm rolling with the Kings and Knights. Jake was spotted during our surveillance and we're going to let him lead us to the top-level players of the operation. This is going down today."

"Something tells me I'm not going to discourage you from going after Jake, especially since you need to be resting."

"No, babe you're not." He hit the side of the car as the agent raised the window.

Waving goodbye, she knew this was the calm before the storm.

Chapter Twenty-One

"These are all pictures of Jake Lowery." Daron shared intel with Mateo who was distracted by his stomach churning, and with thoughts of Rachel and Heaven, as he viewed various images of Jake throughout the years from The Kings' databank. No doubt in his mind that the man on the screen was his partner in crime two decades ago.

He always sensed Jake had a devious side that was prone to cross lines, even the ones drawn by those who controlled the streets, so he never established a friendship away from business. He knew how much Jake could not be trusted, especially after he caught him admiring little girls who were obviously underage.

Looking back, he wondered if Jake was trafficking minors back in the day and only became involved in the child-care system to target more prey. Or maybe after he became involved with children in the foster care system, he decided to use them to earn money on the side.

Either way, it was time for Jake Lowery and everyone who worked with him to spend the rest of their lives behind bars. As he looked out the window and frowned, he decided he would ensure he had the honor of locking him up personally.

"A few other Kings will land in DC in an hour or two," Dro interjected right before they heard a knock at the front door. The three of them looked at each other and Mateo pulled his cell from his pocket and viewed the image from the doorbell security camera.

"I have a feeling you know these dudes on the porch dressed in all black business suits?"

Dro narrowed his eyes and looked at the phone. "Shaz and Reno. They're early. Let 'em in."

Mateo rose and answered the door. "If it's not the men in black."

"Vato, you're funny. You should do stand-up comedy."

"Yes, call me vato, the dude." Mateo welcomed his guests.

"Glad you both got here so soon." Dro gave both men their own custom man-handshakes and hugs.

"Mateo, this is Mariano DeLuca, better known as Reno. He operates the Second Chance at Life Women's Shelter in the Chatham area of Chicago. A place that provides a safe haven for women desiring to escape situations that could possibly cost them their lives." Mateo shook Reno's hand and turned to the second man.

"This is Shastra Bostwick and we call him Shaz. He's a lawyer who fights illegal adoptions and has curtailed the flow of them in the Chicago area.

"Mateo Lopez, and I'm pleased to meet both of you. Have a seat. Can I offer you anything?"

"No, we're good." They settled into the space near Dro who filled them in on details of the investigation thus far while Daron communicated his findings to Mateo.

"I've got eyes on Jake. I probably know more about him than his own parents." Daron smirked.

* * *

An hour passed as they mobilized their plans to not only get Jake, but to take down the entire organization.

"That crew made a mistake when they kidnapped Rachel and Heaven. They're going to pay a high price for it," Reno assured Mateo and the rest of the Kings.

"So, their organization is about to blow up in their faces because they couldn't let fifty thousand dollars go?" Shaz took off his blazer and laid it on the back of one of the dining room chairs.

"On the street, that's a lot of cash," Daron responded.

The Kings had connections in DC and used their intel and tracking systems to determine the location of the other warehouse where Jake and his crew kept the children. Mateo's connection even came through with information regarding a possible transfer that would go down around midnight. They coordinated their findings with Carlos and his associates at the DEA. One way or another, this was ending today.

"Since I'm tapped into the city's electronic grid, we can review traffic in and out of various areas and I can also regulate the city's traffic cameras. They won't know what hit them when they try to get out of there." Daron pinched at his screen to zero in on the second warehouse on one camera and Jake's whereabouts on the other.

Roger, who continued to assist Mateo, had a team staked out at Jake's house, surrounding it from all exit points and they collaborated with the team at Mateo's house, keeping them updated with anything they saw on their end.

Dro walked over to Mateo and touched his shoulder then led him to the kitchen. "Bro, are you good to handle this mission tonight or are you too close to the operation?"

Mateo stepped out of his reach. "I'm going to bring this guy down."

"You know I'm the fixer and people depend on me to do just that." Pausing, he leaned forward, standing toe to toe with Mateo. "Why don't you trust me, get some more rest, and let me and The Kings handle this?"

"No Dro. I'm not letting you count me out." Adrenaline coursed through his body as he heard the commotion of cell phones ringing, large video monitors with incoming notifications pinging, and men carrying iPads and other gadgets to track Jake walking around the room.

"I trust you, but no one and I mean no one, crosses the line with me and harms Rachel." He ran his hand through his hair as he paced in the living room.

He patted Mateo on the back. "I feel you, brother."

"I don't plan to get much sleep until I know that the people who took Rachel and Heaven are behind bars or six feet under."

"Okay, I just wanted to have this talk and remind you we've got your back."

"And so do I."

Mateo's head whipped around at the sound of his brother's voice.

"Juan, did you find something out?" Mateo embraced his brother.

"Guy Brown is the head of this operation and he has major muscle in the city." Juan handed his brother a small piece of paper and some photos. "That's the address to his office and some surveillance photos. It poses as a training center for amateur boxers, but it's where you'll find him. Don't ask me for any details, but I know people who can arrange a meeting if you need it."

Mateo shifted his gaze to the paper. "Muchos gracias. I can't thank you enough."

"We have movement," Daron yelled and sprang into action, hitting and clicking various buttons as the room filled with Roger's voice.

"We've got him and we're staying on him. My connection told me Jake will likely be heading to a couple of warehouses off Florida Avenue near the wholesale shops. He's looking to get paid by a mob boss named Guy Brown for a shipment of kids, then he plans to leave the country. That's the word on the street."

Nervous energy rushed through Mateo's body as he listened. Seconds later, he popped up and began pacing as time ticked away.

* * *

"Let's go." Dro commanded as they quickly gathered their equipment and weapons. "We can head that way and circumvent him going into the warehouse where the kids are kept, after he leads us straight to the others."

Outfitted with Daron's gadgets, they rode in two customized black Ford Expeditions as they made the four-mile drive. They had been waiting at the location about fifteen minutes before Jake's Cadillac Escalade pulled up, facing north. They remained stationed out of Jake's line of sight on the side of the warehouse, as they viewed him through binoculars to track his movements.

When Jake got out of his car alone, Dro and Mateo nodded to each other before proceeding with their mission. Quietly tracking him as he made his way to the side of the building, they observed him enter a code into the keypad next to the door. They slowly moved closer to the entrance, staying well out of sight until Jake disappeared through the door. High above his head the drone, unnoticed, captured images of the long dark steel corridors inside the empty building.

"I have the code," Daron spoke into their ears, as a drone hovering above gathered information. A genius with technology, Daron had invented a drone that was years ahead of commercial grade ones currently on the market. His version had excellent visual and audio capabilities.

Once on the grounds, Dro and Mateo turned on Daron's 'Emperor's Suit' device that caused them to appear camouflaged with the dense foliage surrounding the buildings.

* * *

"What's up Ray-Ray?" Jake greeted a small-framed thug with his pants hanging below his waist.

"Nothing man." Ray-Ray responded.

"Are the connects here?" Jake's eyes shifted from Ray-Ray to the hallway in front.

"Nah, but they should be here shortly. They have the code to the building, and we can go to the office and wait for them."

Dro and Mateo quickly turned off their camouflage suits.

"Go now," Daron spoke into their earpiece after they peeled out of the suits. "Punch in 5-7-3-2." They followed his instructions and the lock released. With the stealth of a jaguar, they continued down the dark hallway to an office at the end of the narrow hall where Jake, Ray-Ray, and Guy Brown were waiting.

"Come in gentlemen." Guy invited Dro and Mateo, who were posing as the connect in the room.

Through his previous affiliations with gangs who ran the streets, Mateo's brother Juan had set up a meeting with authentic connects for the purchase of drugs in the event word got out on the streets about the meeting. Girls were thrown in as a bonus. Juan assured him they would be delayed, but Mateo was worried that the real connects may have been known by someone in Guy's crew. As they entered, Jake narrowed his eyes scrutinizing them, before his eyes rested and stayed on the briefcase Dro carried. Mateo kept his focus on the man in front of him behind the desk.

"Do you have my money?" Guy asked Dro and Mateo as he pulled at his moustache with its distinct cut.

"Listen, we--we... don't want trouble," Ray-Ray stuttered, as Jake attempted to quiet him. "Them girls got away, but I kept my part of the bargain. Me and my crew got them out of that apartment and took them where you wanted them." He quickly answered Guy.

"I have the money right here, but why should I pay you? A deal is a deal and now you're telling me that you don't have the girls." Dro stalled hoping to get more information. A quick look at Mateo and he realized they'd already heard all they needed to implicate Jake. He kept the briefcase he was carrying by his side as he walked closer to Guy's desk, and Mateo remained close to Jake.

"Look, I got them to the warehouse, and I don't know how they got away," he said with a glare in Guy's direction. "These men have the money for the product, and you give them the product. The girls would have been an extra gift, so, we good, right?" Jake tried to move along the negotiations. "Don't worry Guy. I'll find the girls and get your money back."

His worried gaze shifted between Dro and Guy, while Mateo's chest heaved as he recalled Rachel telling him that Jake and his men talked about killing her and Heaven.

He's a double-crossing fool. He probably has no intention of searching for Rachel and Heaven or finding Guy's money.

Mateo had had enough of being in his presence and nodded to Dro that it was time to make their move.

"Rachel is a badass," he said. "That's why she got away."

Jake jerked his head in Mateo's direction and took a swing. Mateo weaved to miss the punch and returned one to his chest, dropping him to the floor. When Dro knocked Ray-Ray out with a swift blow with his briefcase, Guy almost fell out of his chair. A thumping noise from the underside of the desk bounced off the walls as Guy frantically searched for a panic button to summon reinforcements.

"Freeze! Or it will be the last move that you ever make, Guy Brown," Mateo warned.

"How do you know my name?" He continued to hold his hands in the air as he gave them a cold stare. Ray-Ray remained motionless and knocked out from Dro's blow.

"You've been on the FBI's radar for years." Mateo answered, keeping his weapon on him.

"I thought I recognized you." Jake sneered, holding his head as he slowly got up. "Well, well… if it isn't the corner boy turned FBI agent. Get that thing out of my face."

"Shut up Jake," Mateo snapped. "I'm calling the shots now."

Jake scowled as his nostrils flared. "Just like you always thought you did."

"You know him, and yet you brought him into our operation?" Guy's chest heaved, glaring at Jake.

"He sure did," Dro confirmed.

"You know I wouldn't have brought heat down from the FBI. It was stupid Ray-Ray's idea to kidnap the girl, not mine. I only found out after the fact."

"But you knew about it and didn't tell us?" Guy smacked Jake upside the head.

"Listen, the two of you can catch up on old times later." Mateo pointed the gun toward the exit encouraging Guy to get up.

"Let's take a walk outside. We have more to show you," Dro added and they followed them back to the entrance, where to their chagrin, a company of men dressed in black were holding their workers at gunpoint. They rounded up the teenagers and women who had been kidnapped.

"This party is over. You messed with the right one, Jake."

Mateo pushed him in the back, and he fell to the ground in front of his crew who turned their heads as they struggled to hide their laughter. Stretched out on the ground, Jake kissed the dirt and let loose a string of profanity.

Epilogue

Four weeks later...

"Happy birthday to you." Everyone sang in unison as Heaven basked in the glow of her sixteen candles.

"Look at this view. It doesn't get any better than this." Mateo extended his arms toward the Cathedral windows showcasing the five hundred fifty-four feet tall, lighted Washington Monument along with the Lincoln Memorial. The panoramic view of the city was more exquisite than the view from his home and magical as the Christmas lights twinkled like stars.

The POV Restaurant in Upper Northwest Washington, DC, located at the top of the W Hotel, catered to congressmen, senators, and the DC elite. Because of the loveliness of the view, Mateo insisted during their planning, that Heaven's private birthday party start at six thirty in the evening so they would see the beauty of Washington, DC at night.

All the guests had settled into the plush brick red chairs, comfortable after finishing their hearty entrees of seared salmon, juicy ribeye steak, and grilled Maryland crab cakes.

"Who wants cake?" Rachel asked and everyone raised their hands. She turned to Mateo, who raised a finger to signal the waiters. They promptly returned with a knife for Heaven, dessert plates, and forks for all of the invited guests.

"I love a man who can wield power by the wave of a finger. You're our knight, Teo."

Leaning over, she smiled and kissed him as the head waiter placed their plates in front of them and filled their sparkling crystal stems with nonalcoholic bubbly for a toast to Heaven.

"They do that a lot," Heaven laughed, as she shared her observation with the blushing waiter.

Their glasses were filled, and everyone joined in the toast.

"To Heaven," they echoed at the celebration of her sweet sixteenth birthday as she graced them with a beautiful smile and bowed, dressed in her red party dress with a small tiara adorning the top of her head. The Lopez family was all present to share in the joy of Heaven's momentous occasion, and she was forming a fast friendship with Maria and Miguel.

"This has been the best day of my life so far. Thank you, Mama Rachel, and Papi Teo," Heaven said as she placed her Shirley Temple on the table after taking a sip. "I look at the two of you and I feel like I'm the luckiest girl in the world." She paused and looked at those in attendance.

"When I look up at the sky tonight, I see three stars twinkling so bright, that I know it has to be my Mom, Justice, and Caleb shining down on me from heaven.

Rachel averted her gaze momentarily to the ceiling, ignoring the tears welling up in her eyes.

"My biological mother always told us kids that God gave each of us a gift, but I thought maybe he forgot about me." Her shoulders slumped as if the words carried too much weight. "Until I was talking to my therapist and she told me that Teo means God or gift from God in Spanish. I—" Holding her chest, she tried swallowing the lump in her throat but Rachel and Teo rose and brought her into a group hug.

A few others grabbed their napkins or used their hands to wipe tears.

Mateo looked into the teen's eyes and exclaimed, "Gracias, Heaven for the kind words but let me remind you that your gift was always within you." Drying her eyes, she blinked and looked at him in disbelief.

"What do you mean?" Her voice was low and tentative after giving breath to her wounds and allowing others to see and feel it.

"What is your name?" Mateo held Heaven's hand.

"Heaven Hart, you know my name." She rolled her eyes and smirked.

"That was your gift, Heaven." Mateo pointed to her heart. "You're the girl full of heart, courage, and compassion. That's what I felt the moment I met you."

Heaven patted her eyes then looked up and grinned.

"Do you want to thank your guests for coming to celebrate with us?"

She nodded before round two of tears began falling and accepted their hands as

they led her to the front of the room. Teo handed her the mic and she thanked everyone for coming to her party and for all the presents it would take her hours to open. Next, she handed the mic to Rachel to speak.

"Thank you everyone, our extended family, for all you've done to help us through this challenge." She smiled and gazed around the room at the Lopez family, Lachelle, John and their girls, members of The Kings, and employees of Mateo's company. Then it was Mateo's turn at the mic. He startled her by requesting her attention as members of the wait staff provided her with a high back ornately decorated chair fit for a queen.

"Rachel, this one is for you." Stroking her shoulders, he began singing to the karaoke version of *All I Want for Christmas* as she smiled throughout his rendition.

"Bro, don't quit your day job," Dro joked from a few seats away.

"Don't laugh at my man," Rachel admonished Dro as Mateo puffed out his chest, strutting like a peacock.

Working with the Kings and the Knights gave him the push he needed to retire and take the plunge into becoming a full-time entrepreneur, Founder and CEO of Global Connection Security, LLC. He offered his brother a contract to service the fleet of vehicles he planned to buy that would be needing regular maintenance and to give him a way to distance himself from the darker parts of his life.

"I always wanted to expand my business. This will give me the capital I've always needed." The two brothers had sealed the deal with a hug two days ago.

Jake, Ray-Ray, and Guy were arrested and held without bond on a gamut of federal charges ranging from sex trafficking, drug distribution, and selling guns. Jake tried to obtain a deal by telling Mateo that he tried to get Rachel focused on a case in South Carolina and it was her decision to continue to investigate the Hart case, not his.

"This isn't deal worthy," Mateo told his supervisors after he conferred with Rachel and Heaven.

The Kings and Knights assisted in securing housing and wrap-around services for the women and children that were freed, and the fifty thousand dollars Heaven took from the warehouse and stuffed in her bag was found in Rachel's apartment and given to the authorities.

The tone got serious when Mateo glanced at the table with his old friends Carlos, and Dro with his lady, then at his new friends Daron, Shaz, and Reno and their women, as well.

"I want to thank our family, The Kings and Knights, for flying back into town to join us in celebrating Heaven's sixteenth birthday." A smile lifted his lips. "The last few weeks have been a whirlwind, and through it all, we've created a connection that will last a lifetime."

Their guests let out a collective 'awwww'.

He looked down and gazed into Rachel's eyes.

"Sweetheart, will you join me?"

Rachel stood, and like a magnet, was drawn into Mateo's embrace.

"If anyone told me a few months ago that I'd meet a woman with your passion for giving to others, strength to care for those who matter to you, and fortitude to never give up, I would have never believed them." He unbuttoned his jacket. "In the presence of all those gathered today, I'm making a public declaration that I never intend to leave your side." Then he lowered to one knee and took the small red leather jewelry box from Heaven.

"Rachel…will you marry me and be my forever lady?"

She fixed her gaze on Heaven. "You knew about this and didn't tell me?"

"Yes, so please answer Papi Mateo before his knees give out on him."

"Yes…yes, I will be honored to be your wife." She beamed as he rose and took her into his arms kissing her to the cheers of all those in the room and then turned to Heaven.

"Come here mija, my daughter."

He embraced her, admiring her with the pride of a father, and then Rachel as the woman he adored and loved more than life itself.

Flexing her fingers, she admired her newest piece of jewelry twinkling as the lights in the room bounced off the flawless three carat, round cut, diamond mounted in platinum.

"You're blinding us Rachel," Carlos yelled from the rear and everyone laughed.

"I love it, Teo. Thank you for making this one of the happiest days of my life." She placed her left hand on her chest as their guest shielded their eyes, pretending they were blinded by the light.

"Your happiness is my happiness, my queen."

He bowed to her and then adjusted his black tie matching his brand new all black tailor-made designer suit, accented with his crisp white shirt. Pulling Rachel and Heaven onto the dance floor, he pantomimed JT from Kool and the Gang while the DJ began spinning Celebration.

The entire dinner party joined the hosts and the birthday girl in celebrating happiness and new-found beginnings with champagne flowing from fountains around the room.

Over the next few weeks, not a day went by without them spending time either at Rachel's or Mateo's home over dinner. Rachel received approval to become a foster parent for Heaven, and with high hopes they started the adoption process to make them a forever family. Mateo couldn't imagine his world without his awesome woman at his side, a smart teenager as a future daughter, and his new-found brothers.

Looking forward to the time ahead which was beyond his wildest imagination, he prayed their days would be filled with love and happiness.

About the Knights of the Castle Series

Don't miss the hot new standalone series. The Kings of the Castle made them family, but the Knights will transform the world.

Book 1 - King of Durabia – Naleighna Kai

No good deed goes unpunished, or that's how Ellena Kiley feels after she rescues a child and the former Crown Prince of Durabia offers to marry her.

Kamran learns of a nefarious plot to undermine his position with the Sheikh and jeopardize his ascent to the throne. He's unsure how Ellena, the fiery American seductress, fits into the plan but she's a secret weapon he's unwilling to relinquish.

Ellena is considered a sister by the Kings of the Castle and her connection to Kamran challenges her ideals, her freedoms, and her heart. Plus, loving him makes her a potential target for his enemies. When Ellena is kidnapped, Kamran is forced to bring in the Kings.

In the race against time to rescue his woman and defeat his enemies, the kingdom of Durabia will never be the same.

Book 2 - Knight of Bronzeville – Naleighna Kai and Stephanie M. Freeman

Chaz Maharaj thought he could maintain the lie of a perfect marriage for his adoring fans … until he met Amanda.

The connection between them should have ended with that unconditional "hall pass" which led to one night of unbridled passion. But once would never satisfy his hunger for a woman who could never be his. When Amanda walked out of his life, it was supposed to be forever. Neither of them could have anticipated fate's plan.

Chaz wants to explore his feelings for Amanda, but Susan has other ideas. Prepared to fight for his budding romance and navigate a plot that's been laid to crush them, an unexpected twist threatens his love and her life.

When Amanda's past comes back to haunt them, Chaz enlists the Kings of the Castle to save his newfound love in a daring escape.

Book 3 - Knight of South Holland – Karen D. Bradley

He's a brilliant inventor, but he'll decimate anyone who threatens his woman.

When the Kings of the Castle recommend Calvin Atwood, strategic defense inventor, to create a security shield for the kingdom of Durabia, it's the opportunity of a lifetime. The only problem—it's a two-year assignment and he promised his fiancée they would step away from their dangerous lifestyle and start a family.

Security specialist, Mia Jakob, adores Calvin with all her heart, but his last assignment put both of their lives at risk. She understands how important this new role is to the man she loves, but the thought that he may be avoiding commitment does cross her mind.

Calvin was sure he'd made the best decision for his and Mia's future, until enemies of the state target his invention and his woman. Set on a collision course with hidden foes, this Knight will need the help of the Kings to save both his Queen and the Kingdom of Durabia.

Book 4 - Lady of Jeffrey Manor – J. S. Cole and Naleighna Kai

He's the kingdom's most eligible bachelor. She's a practical woman on temporary assignment.

When surgical nurse, Blair Swanson, departed the American Midwest for an assignment in the Kingdom of Durabia she had no intention of finding love.

As a member of the Royal Family, Crown Prince Hassan has a responsibility to the throne. A loveless, arranged marriage is his duty, but the courageous American nurse is his desire.

When a dark secret threatens everything Hassan holds dear, how will he fulfill his royal duty and save the lady who holds his heart?

Book 5 - Knight of Grand Crossing – Hiram Shogun Harris, Naleighna Kai, and Anita L. Roseboro

Rahm did time for a crime he didn't commit. Now that he's free, taking care of the three women who supported him on a hellish journey is his priority, but old enemies are waiting in the shadows.

Rahm Fosten's dream life as a Knight of the Castle includes Marilyn Spears, who quiets the injustice of his rough past, but in his absence a new foe has infiltrated his family.

Marilyn Spears waited for many years to have someone like Rahm in her life. Now that he's home, an unexpected twist threatens to rip him away again. As much as she loves him, she's not willing to go where this new drama may lead.

Meanwhile, Rahm's gift to his Aunt Alyssa brings her to Durabia, where she catches the attention of wealthy surgeon, Ahmad Maharaj. Her attendance at a private Bliss event puts her under his watchful eye, but also in the crosshairs of the worst kind of enemy. Definitely the wrong timing for the rest of the challenges Rahm is facing.

While Rahm and Marilyn navigate their romance, a deadly threat has him and the Kings of the Castle primed to keep Marilyn, Alyssa, and his family from falling prey to an adversary out for bloody revenge.

Book 6 - Knight of Paradise Island – J. L. Campbell

Someone is killing women and the villain's next target strikes too close to the Kingdom of Durabia.

Dorian "Ryan" Bostwick is a protector and he's one of the best in the business. When a King of the Castle assigns him to find his former lover, Aziza, he stumbles upon a deadly underworld operating close to the Durabian border.

Aziza Hampton had just rekindled her love affair with Ryan when a night out with friends ends in her kidnapping. Alone and scared, she must find a way to escape her captor and reunite with her lover.

In a race against time, Ryan and the Kings of the Castle follow ominous clues into the underbelly of a system designed to take advantage of the vulnerable. Failure isn't an option and Ryan will rain down hell on earth to save the woman of his heart.

Book 7 - Knight of Irondale – J. L Woodson, Naleighna Kai, and Martha Kennerson

Neesha Carpenter is on the run from a stalker ex-boyfriend, so why are the police hot on her trail?

Neesha escaped the madness of her previous relationship only to discover the Chicago Police have named her the prime suspect in her ex's shooting. With her life spinning out of control, she turns to the one man who's the biggest threat to her heart—Christian Vidal, her high school sweetheart.

Christian has always been smitten with Neesha's strength, intelligence and beauty. He offers her safe haven in the kingdom of Durabia and will do whatever it takes to keep her safe, even enlisting the help of the Kings of the Castle.

Neesha and Christian's rekindled flame burns hotter even as her stay in the country places the Royal Family at odds with the American government.

As mounting evidence points to Neesha's guilt, Christian must ask the hard question … is the woman he loves being framed or did she pull the trigger?

Book 8 - Knight of Birmingham – Lori Hays and MarZe Scott

Single mothers who are eligible for release, have totally disappeared from the Alabama justice system.

Women's advocate, Meghan Turner, has uncovered a disturbing pattern and she's desperate for help. Then her worse nightmare becomes a horrific reality when her friend goes missing under the same mysterious circumstances.

Rory Tannous has spent his life helping society's most vulnerable. When he learns of Meghan's dilemma, he takes it personal. Rory has his own tragic past and he'll utilize every connection, even the King of the Castle, to help this intriguing woman find her friend and the other women.

As Rory and Meghan work together, the attraction grows and so does the danger. The stakes are high and they will have to risk their love and lives to defeat a powerful adversary.

Book 9 - Knight of Penn Quarter – Terri Ann Johnson and Michele Sims

Following an undercover FBI sting operation that didn't go as planned, Agent Mateo Lopez is ready to put the government agency in his rearview mirror.

A confirmed workaholic, his career soared at the cost of his love life which had crashed and burned until mutual friends arranged a date with beautiful, sharp-witted, Rachel Jordan, a rising star at a children's social services agency.

Unlucky in love, Rachel has sworn off romantic relationships, but Mateo finds himself falling for her in more ways than one. When trouble brews in one of Rachel's cases, he does everything in his power to keep her safe—even if it means resorting to extreme measures.

Will the choices they make bring them closer together or cost them their lives?

About the Kings of the Castle Series

"Did you miss The Kings of the Castle? "They are so expertly crafted and flow so well between each of the books, it's hard to tell each is crafted by a different author. Very well done!" - Lori H…, Amazon and Goodreads

Each King book 2-9 is a standalone, NO cliffhangers

Book 1 – Kings of the Castle, the introduction to the series and story of King of Wilmette (Vikkas Germaine)

USA TODAY, New York Times, and National Bestselling Authors

work together to provide you with a world you'll never want to leave. The Castle.

Fate made them brothers, but protecting the Castle, each other, and the women they love, will make them Kings. Their combined efforts to find the current Castle members responsible for the attempt on their mentor's life, is the beginning of dangerous challenges that will alter the path of their lives forever.

These powerful men, unexpectedly brought together by their pasts and current circumstances, will become a force to be reckoned with.

King of Chatham - Book 2 – London St. Charles

While Mariano "Reno" DeLuca uses his skills and resources to create safe havens for battered women, a surge in criminal activity within the Chatham area threatens the women's anonymity and security. When Zuri, an exotic Tanzanian Princess, arrives seeking refuge from an arranged marriage and its deadly consequences, Reno is now forced to relocate the women in the shelter, fend off unforeseen enemies of The Castle, and endeavor not to lose his heart to the mysterious woman.

King of Evanston - Book 3 - J. L. Campbell

Raised as an immigrant, he knows the heartache of family separation firsthand. His personal goals and business ethics collide when a vulnerable woman stands to lose her baby in an underhanded and profitable scheme crafted by powerful, ruthless businessmen and politicians who have nefarious ties to The Castle. Shaz and the Kings of the Castle collaborate to uproot the dark forces intent on changing the balance of power within The Castle and destroying their mentor. National Bestselling Author, J.L. Campbell presents book 3 in the Kings of the Castle Series, featuring Shaz Bostwick.

King of Devon - Book 4 - Naleighna Kai

When a coma patient becomes pregnant, Jaidev Maharaj's medical facility comes under a government microscope and media scrutiny. In the midst of the investigation, he receives a mysterious call from someone in his past that demands that more of him than he's ever been willing to give and is made aware of a dark family secret that will destroy the people he loves most.

King of Morgan Park - Book 5 - Karen D. Bradley

Two things threaten to destroy several areas of Daron Kincaid's life—the tracking device he developed to locate victims of sex trafficking and an inherited membership in a mysterious outfit called The Castle. The new developments set the stage to dismantle the relationship with a woman who's been trained to make men weak or put them on the other side of the grave. The secrets Daron keeps from Cameron and his inner circle only complicates an already tumultuous situation caused by an FBI sting that brought down his former enemies. Can Daron take on his enemies, manage his secrets and loyalty to the Castle without permanently losing the woman he loves?

King of South Shore - Book 6 - MarZe Scott

Award-winning real estate developer, Kaleb Valentine, is known for turning failing communities into thriving havens in the Metro Detroit area. His plans to rebuild his hometown neighborhood are derailed with one phone call that puts Kaleb deep in the middle of an intense criminal investigation led by a detective who has a personal vendetta. Now he will have to deal with the ghosts of his past before they kill him.

King of Lincoln Park - Book 7 – Martha Kennerson

Grant Khambrel is a sexy, successful architect with big plans to expand his Texas Company. Unfortunately, a dark secret from his past could destroy it all unless he's willing to betray the man responsible for that success, and the woman who becomes the key to his salvation.

King of Hyde Park - Book 8 -Lisa Dodson

Alejandro "Dro" Reyes has been a "fixer" for as long as he could remember, which makes owning a crisis management company focused on repairing professional reputations the perfect fit. The same could be said of Lola Samuels, who is only vaguely aware of his "true" talents and seems to be oblivious to the growing attraction between them. His company, Vantage Point, is in high demand and business in the Windy City is booming. Until a mysterious call following an attempt on his mentor's life forces him to drop everything and accept a fated position with The Castle. But there's a hidden agenda and unexpected enemy that Alejandro doesn't see coming who threatens his life, his woman, and his throne.

King of Lawndale - Book 9 - Janice M. Allen

Dwayne Harper's passion is giving disadvantaged boys the tools to transform themselves into successful men. Unfortunately, the minute he steps up to take his place among the men he considers brothers, two things stand in his way: a political office that does not want the competition Dwayne's new education system will bring, and a well-connected former member of The Castle who will use everything in his power—even those who Dwayne mentors—to shut him down.

Terri Ann Johnson is an award-winning author for her debut novel, Faith Alone. She writes books with hope exploding from the pages through tragedy, adversity and triumph. The national bestselling author expertly spotlights everyday people embroiled in not-so-ordinary circumstances with wisdom and compassion; her focus on faith, forgiveness and restoration not only allows readers to get lost between the pages but be inspired by them.

If you enjoyed Knight of Penn Quarter and would like to find out more about Lachelle and John, Rachel and Mateo's friends, please download or purchase a copy of my award-winning debut novel, Faith Alone.

www.terriannjohnson.com

Author **Michele Sims** is the creator of the Moore Family Saga. She loves writing hot love stories and women's fiction in multigenerational families. She is the recipient of the 2019 RSJ Debut Author Award, the 2018 RSJ Aspiring Author Award, and first runner up in the Introvert Press Poetry Contest for February 2018. She is a member of the LRWA, in Charleston, SC. She lives in South Carolina with her husband who has been her soulmate and greatest cheerleader. She is the proud mother of two adult sons and the auntie to many loved ones. When she's not writing, she's trying to remember the importance of exercise, travelling, listening to different genres of music, and observing the wonders of life on this marvelous planet.

www.authormichelesims.com